THE FINAL SPIRE

'Mystery Mountain' Mania in the 1930s

Other books by Trevor Marc Hughes

Nearly 40 on the 37: Triumph and Trepidation on the Stewart–Cassiar Highway, 2013

Zero Avenue to Peace Park: Confidence and Collapse on the 49th Parallel, 2016

Capturing the Summit: Hamilton Mack Laing and the Mount Logan Expedition of 1925, 2023

As editor

Riding the Continent: Hamilton Mack Laing, 2019

THE FINAL SPIRE

TREVOR MARC HUGHES

'Mystery Mountain' Mania in the 1930s

Ronsdale Press

THE FINAL SPIRE
Copyright © 2025 Trevor Marc Hughes

RONSDALE PRESS
125A – 1030 Denman Street, Vancouver, B.C. Canada V6G 2M6
www.ronsdalepress.com

Book Design: Derek von Essen
Cover Design: Dorian Danielsen

Ronsdale Press wishes to thank the following for their support of its publishing program: the Canada Council for the Arts, the Government of Canada, the British Columbia Arts Council, and the Province of British Columbia through the British Columbia Book Publishing Tax Credit program.

LIBRARY AND ARCHIVES CANADA CATALOGUING IN PUBLICATION

Title: The final spire : 'Mystery Mountain' mania in the 1930s / Trevor Marc Hughes.
Names: Hughes, Trevor Marc, 1972- author
Description: Includes bibliographical references and index.
Identifiers: Canadiana (print) 20250109360 | Canadiana (ebook) 20250109425 | ISBN 9781553807223 (softcover) | ISBN 9781553807230 (EPUB)
Subjects: LCSH: Mountaineers—Travel—British Columbia—Waddington, Mount. | LCSH: Mountaineering—
British Columbia—Waddington, Mount. | LCSH: Mountaineers—Manitoba—History. | LCSH: Waddington,
Mount (B.C.)—Description and travel.
Classification: LCC FC3845.W33 H84 2025 | DDC 917.11/103—dc23

At Ronsdale Press we are committed to protecting the environment. To this end we are working with Canopy and printers to phase out our use of paper produced from ancient forests. This book is one step towards that goal.

Printed in Canada

To the Alpine Club of Canada, Vancouver Section,
and the British Columbia Mountaineering Club

CONTENTS

ACKNOWLEDGEMENTS

would like to acknowledge that much of the story of this book takes place on the traditional and unceded territory of the Xwémalhkwu, or Homalco People, which neighbours the territory of the Tŝilhqot'in People just over the mountains to the east.

The mountain once called Mystery Mountain in the days of the initial climbs of Don and Phyllis Munday, and later referred to as Mount Waddington by expeditions, including that of the Neave brothers, has a traditional Homalco name: Xwe7xw. The traditional and unceded territory of the Xwémalhkwu "stretches from south of Hornby Island, west through Johnstone Strait, north to Tatla Lake and east to Bishop River," according to the Homalco First Nation's website.[1] "Native Indians of British Columbia are known to have used the valley of the Homathko river as a travel route between the head of Bute Inlet and the Interior long before the advent of the white man. They were still using it until the end of the 1880s," spoke mountaineer Dr. Neal M. Carter in 1964."[2]

For more information about the Xwémalhkwu, or Homalco People, and traditional place names, visit https://www.homalco.com.

3

In addition, my thanks go to Richard Mackie for introducing me to the writings of Hamilton Mack Laing, whose work with mountaineers led me to the extraordinary tales of Mystery Mountain.

Thanks to Paul Geddes of the Alpine Club of Canada, Vancouver Section, who introduced me to the Archives of North Vancouver, and archivists Georgia Twiss and Rebecca Pasch. Many a Friday research trip was made there through 2023 and into 2024. Thanks, Georgia and Rebecca, for making my life easier by providing me with insight and boxes of *The B.C. Mountaineer* to look through. Thanks also to Graeme Niedtner for scanning in the Don Munday sketch maps.

Thanks to Kathryn Bridge, who introduced me to Katy Hughes at the BC Archives. This was instrumental in a brief but productive visit to Victoria in which I found much useful photography of the Munday expeditions, as well as audio files of Phyl Munday and Roger Neave that fleshed out their respective expeditions throughout those heady years of pilgrimages to the southern peaks of the Coast Range. Thanks also to Katy Hughes herself, who taught me a great many things about the multiple systems that come together, or sometimes don't, to make up an archive.

Thanks to my wife, Laura, and to my sons, Michael and Marc, for their support and love.

Last but certainly not least, I must thank all at Ronsdale Press, including Wendy Atkinson, Kevin Welsh, editor Arlene Prunkl, cover designer Dorian Danielsen, and book designer Derek von Essen for their tremendous help in getting this book published.

PREFACE

n November 2023, I found myself walking down the icy driveway of the Juniper Hotel with a free afternoon. I had come to Banff not only to attend the Alpine Club of Canada's Mountain Guides Ball at the Banff Springs Hotel, but also to take in some of the events of the Banff Mountain Book Competition. While there, I took time to create awareness of *Capturing the Summit*, my recent title about the Mount Logan expedition of 1925. I had driven the twelve-hour trip from Vancouver in one stretch and hadn't had much exercise since, so I needed a walk. My legs would have a stretch and my lungs take in plenty of fresh mountain air on my half-hour stroll before I reached the doors of the Whyte Museum and Archives in town.

I was greeted by archivist Kayla Cazes, who guided me in for my research appointment. As I did not get to Banff very often, I decided to pick up from where I'd left off in my *Capturing the Summit* research and do some further reading into the expedition records of the Alpine Club of Canada. Before I stepped into the research room, I heard the entrance door open once again and another figure came in from the cold. When he removed his toque, I recognized him instantly from his friendly manner and deep voice. I'd met mountaineer and historian Chic Scott at the Mountain Guides Ball just a few nights before, and I'd shown him a copy of my new book. He was a regular at the archives, most recently working on an overview of the Alpine Club of Canada, a major work of mountaineering history. After we exchanged greetings and took our seats at two nearby tables, Kayla wheeled out a trolley containing issues of the *Canadian Alpine Journal* going back to 1908, pushing it to where Mr. Scott was seated. It seemed like an omen of sorts to see him again, and I now felt confident that I'd come to right place for my Canadian mountaineering history research, not to mention chuffed that I'd be doing my own searching, albeit without as much direction as him, just a short distance away.

My further perusal of the expedition records after 1925, where I'd left off a few years ago, brought me into contact with some of the earliest photography of the expeditions of the Alpine Club of Canada. Black-and-white photographs from climbs on Vancouver Island and the Rockies appeared before me. When I came across the group photograph from the 1906 founding meeting of the Alpine Club of Canada in Winnipeg, in which appeared founders Elizabeth Parker and A.O. Wheeler, I couldn't contain my schoolboy enthusiasm, and I had to show it to Mr. Scott. "Look what I found," I whispered. We shared a smile and he acknowledged its importance to the mountaineering community. This photograph represented the earliest days of mountaineering in Canada, and to have noted that with Chic Scott was an auspicious start to any project that might come out of my research. I was in good company.

After an hour, I came across a folder, inside of which was a piece of notepad paper and a very worn diary. The paper was dated, written in cursive with a pen, "Thursday, Aug. 16th, 1979." Beneath this was written a brief statement:

> *Dear Gil,*
>
> *Here is the Waddington trip diary. Some of it is a bit travel worn, and hard to read, so you may have to do some guessing.*
>
> *Best Regards,*
> *Roger*

Ferris Neave's diary and the note that was found inside.

The diary's leather cover had been torn, creased, and scratched, the edges scuffed. Opening it, I read on the first inside page words etched in fading pencil:

Waddington Expedition
1934
(F. Neave)

I believe the note was in the handwriting of Roger Neave, brother of Ferris Neave, both of whom attempted the final tower of Mount Waddington in 1934 with Campbell Secord. By 1979, the date written at the top of the notepad paper, Roger had already been president of the Alpine Club of Canada (in 1967 and 1968), and he was climbing with Gilbert "Gil" Parker. He had made an attempt on Mount Noel with Parker in the Stikine Region of B.C. in 1977, a climb led by Rafe Hutchinson.

As I turned the delicate pages, I noted that even though the pencil writing was fading and in some places was smudged and illegible, the record of this 1934 expedition was otherwise in good condition. This in itself was valuable. My researcher's instincts had been tantalized by seeing there was much more to read about this expedition to Mount Waddington, which, at 4,019 metres (13,186 feet), is the tallest mountain within the boundaries of British Columbia. At my book launch for *Capturing the Summit* in Courtenay on Vancouver Island in June 2023, I'd had an animated conversation with an American man about which was the tallest mountain in British Columbia, Mount Waddington or Mount Fairweather. Fairweather is taller than Waddington, but it is situated partially in British Columbia and partially in Alaska.

My involvement with the Alpine Club of Canada, Vancouver Section, had grown since the publication of *Capturing the Summit*. In March 2023, prior to its publication, I met via Zoom with club section members Paul Geddes, Liz Scremin, and Richa Chuttani and chatted with them about Mount Logan. The new association with the Alpine Club of Canada struck me as being important, and I was glad to have made that connection.

Not long after my return to Vancouver, I began attending the local section's meetings, and Paul Geddes introduced me to the British

Columbia Mountaineering Club Fonds at the Archives of North Vancouver. The modest former elementary school building in Lynn Valley houses a great deal of the mountaineering lore of the province, and soon I was tucking into early copies of *The BC Mountaineer*, the regular publication of the BCMC. I began learning more about an active mountaineering community in Vancouver a century ago that explored the North Shore mountains, inspired by European tradition, and was hungry to climb more remote peaks in the Coast Range. Don and Phyllis Munday were key in promoting exciting mountaineering opportunities. Without the Mundays, the celebrity mountaineering couple of their day, Mystery Mountain mania would not likely have exploded the way it did in the 1920s and 1930s.

When I began writing *The Final Spire*, I had planned to tell the story of Ferris and Roger Neave, Campbell Secord, and Arthur Davidson—their road trip from Winnipeg and their trudge from Tatlayoko Lake and attempt on Mount Waddington from the east along Tiedemann Glacier, the route most often used by mountaineers attempting the peak today. But I could not simply jump into the story of the quartet of mountaineers piling into Ferris Neave's 1930 Plymouth without describing the route exploration already done by Don and Phyllis Munday from 1925 onward. It soon became apparent in my research that, not unlike in *Capturing the Summit*, in which, even though the naturalist's story was at the core I could not resist telling the story of the mountaineers, I could not resist in *The Final Spire* describing the backstory of why four young men from Winnipeg had the spirit to make the difficult journey to Waddington. Not only did they drive to Tatalyoko Lake, taking on poor roads and muddy terrain, but they also challenged themselves to cross forbidding creeks, row vast lakes, and traverse glaciers before even getting a crack at the tallest mountain in British Columbia. What had ignited their passion for this ominous peak?

In the course of the story appear the tremendous figures who, in a very active decade, all furthered the understanding of an incredibly remote and treacherous place. They were drawn not only to a nightmarish rock tower encased in ice and snow, but also to both the solace and the challenge of the expedition. Phyllis Munday, Don Munday, Neal M. Carter, Alec Dalgleish, Ferris Neave, Roger Neave, Cam Secord,

A.A. McCoubrey, and many more individuals were a part of the pilgrimages to the final spire of British Columbia.

In *Capturing the Summit* I explained that I was not a mountaineer. After submitting a first draft of this manuscript in October 2024, I decided to try the sport I had written so passionately about. Partially I needed to break out of my sedentary writer lifestyle. But my primary motivation was that I was drawn anew to the North Shore mountains after having read and written about Don and Phyllis Munday; they'd had a cabin on the shoulder of Dam Mountain in the 1920s. On a mild day in October, I made for the peak, which stands at 1,349 metres (4,426 feet), climbing through a recent dusting of snow, hauling myself up through the meltwater and mud, testing my footing before committing to a step. At last I summitted the conical, clouded peak, elated, lungs filled with fresh air. I sat there with the peak to myself, appreciating my surroundings as I nibbled on some trail mix and experiencing, in a small way, what those pioneer mountaineers had.

Trevor Marc Hughes
Vancouver, British Columbia
November 12, 2024

INTRODUCTION:
THE INNER SPIRIT

Here . . . was the real glory; that, half conquerors, half pilgrims, they were able to stride into the darkness with a confidence found in the Alps, hoping that they yet might find some all-embracing belief that had eluded both them and the age through which they had thundered.

—Ronald Clark, *The Victorian Mountaineers*

During what has been called by historians a "golden age," Victorian mountaineers flocked to the Alps. Among the young men who made the pilgrimage during the 1850s and 1860s to the peaks of the Monte Rosa massif, including the death-defying Matterhorn, were the brash Edward Whymper, the inquiring James David Forbes, thinkers such as John Ruskin, and the men of spiritual belief such as Charles Hudson. These men, predominantly from Britain, increasingly followed the well-worn trail from London to the great peaks of the Alps. This golden age, described by historian and author Ronald Clark as having "started with the conquest of the Wetterhorn by Alfred Wills in 1854 and ended with the ascent of the Matterhorn by Whymper and his party in 1865,"[1] came out of a time of material wealth, building momentum through years of increasing industrialization. It was a time of peace, economic well-being, and of leisure time for a certain elite group. It could be said that mountaineering's growth as a sport emanated from this period of wealth and privilege, and circumstances had men wishing to prove themselves, perhaps even escape an industrialized world of their own creation. But the obsession of all climbers can't be understood with this simple explanation. What extracted men from their comfortable surroundings and motivated them to take on the risks and dangers inherent in the mountains? What was it about this Mecca of the Alps that was the focus of this attention? Ronald Clark has this to say: "The Victorians were always asking questions and they climbed, fundamentally, because they wanted their questions answered. ... It is no coincidence that scientists and clergymen were so numerous among the early mountaineers."[2]

John Ruskin

Thinkers such as John Ruskin, although not inclined to be mountaineers themselves, described with feeling the aesthetic of the mountains, changing the paradigm of mountains as forbidden places to explore. For Ruskin, "the mountains were examples of God's handiwork and in moving among them man could learn to discover himself."[3] His writing inclined young men of the age towards the peaks, but they were also a new draw among professionals, geologists, philosophers, and men of the cloth. These adventurers sought inquiry among the spires of the Alps, in search of what the industrial world could not give them. Clark explains:

> Some climbed because they desired to explore, and the Alps formed the most convenient field for their exploration. Some climbed "for the exercise." Some climbed for a sight of the majestic scenery which could not be viewed, as Ruskin had imagined, from the bottom of the mountains. Yet the common denominator, which could be seen more clearly as the century progressed, lay outside the realm of material experience. It lay, rather, in the realm of the inner spirit, enclosed in a dissatisfaction with the great material satisfaction of the age, a dissatisfaction which it was rarely possible and even more rarely expedient to express.[4]

In 1865, the Matterhorn was first climbed by a group that set out from the town of Zermatt, which the spire-like tower of the mountain overlooks. This climbing party comprised Lord Francis Douglas, Douglas Hadow, guides Michel Croz and Peter Taugwalder (with Taugwalder's two sons as porters), Charles Hudson, an accomplished man of the mountains and spiritual leader who had served as a chaplain in the Crimea, and the brash, confident Edward Whymper. Not unlike the deeply spiritual men of the time who came to the mountains year after year such as Leslie Stephen and Hereford Brooke George, Charles Hudson, who would die on the Matterhorn in 1865, sought, in a growing age of science in which beliefs were increasingly questioned, solace in the heights, in sights that defied description and created an epiphany of the soul. Both scientists and clergymen found similar reasons for ascending the great heights; it is possible the former had too much certainty and knowing in their lives while the latter were too familiar with the codified rituals in their worshipful practices. Both geologists and clergymen headed for the hills with similar goals in mind—to find "deep spiritual satisfaction."[5] When scientific practices eroded spiritual foundations, including the belief of everlasting life and a limited cosmological view, a new kind of spiritual practice emerged. This gets into the crux of the origins of mountaineering: "The real seed of mountain-worship—when immortality goes, hold fast to the magnificent certainties of mountain-form and mountain-beauty."[6]

Yet this beauty could be deceptive. That search for the aesthetic that brought men escaping their comfortable Victorian surroundings for the risks inherent in the Alps could bring glory, or it could bring death. In the enthusiasm of Whymper and the lore that surrounded that first glory on the Matterhorn that met with tragedy in the death of four men was the culmination of an age, embodied by the church-like spire of the peak. In this imagery of high, seemingly inaccessible, perhaps even forbidden peaks lay mystery. "Many Victorian Churchmen realised the fact," Ronald Clark wrote. "And, after the physical circumstances of the age had persuaded them up into the mountains, they found on them some hint of this mystic and needed link between themselves and the unexplained and the inexplicable."[7] As John Ruskin put it, when it came to the mountains: "They seem to have been built for the human race, as at once their schools and cathedrals; full of treasures of illuminated manuscript for the scholar, kindly in simple lessons to the worker, quiet in pale cloisters for the thinker, glorious in holiness for the worshipper."[8]

There were scientists such as James David Forbes, an Edinburgh University professor with a decidedly spiritual bent, whose mountain adventures featured "the same unusual mixture of intellectual observation and emotional enjoyment" that gave the age "the ideal example of the transformation which so often took place in those scientists who came to the mountains to study and who stayed to worship."[9]

Men of worship such as clergyman Charles Hudson were accomplished mountaineers. As Ronald Clark noted, "It is difficult to discover any aspect of Victorian climbing in which some cleric does not play an important part."[10] Hudson was credited for more of the success of the first ascent of the Matterhorn than anyone else except Edward Whymper, who was part of the climb. Hudson was a tenacious, serious climber,

Zermatt, Switzerland, in the late nineteenth century. Many attempts on the Matterhorn, which looms in the background, were launched from the town.

and a tenacious, serious man. For him, the challenges of the age were "problems which the growing knowledge of science was creating" and through his climbing he found "some solace from the troubles of the world that was something more than mere escapism."[11] He would join Whymper in Zermatt in 1865 for that extraordinary climb of the Matterhorn. Edward Whymper, by trade an artist and engraver, made attempts on the Matterhorn every season from 1861 to 1865. His profession had brought him to the Alps, with William Longman of Longman, Green, Longman, and Roberts, who requested that Whymper "prepare a series of sketches for the coming volume of *Peaks, Passes and Glaciers* which was then in course of preparation."[12] Ronald Clark wrote, "Whymper climbed for none of the mixed moral reasons that moved his contemporaries. He saw mountains clearly and without qualification as a challenge to man's supremacy."[13] In 1861, it was generally thought that "the majority of mountaineers still considered that it [the Matterhorn] was not only inaccessible but that it would remain so."[14] If anything, this knowledge seemed to fuel Whymper all the more. In the 1862 season, he experienced four defeats during four attempts at the peak, which caused him to brood and think of the next approach.[15] In 1863, he made a sixth attempt for the prize, but was stopped by weather conditions. He was indeed "relentless in his assault on rocks" and would continue to be so.[16] His 1865 attempt was successful, but it was shrouded by the deaths of Croz, Hadow, Hudson, and Douglas that occurred on the descent.

> A few hundred feet down they reached the steepest part of their route. The slabs were dangerous but not inherently difficult, although in the circumstances they must have been difficult enough. At one point, Croz turned to guide Hadow's feet into the best positions on the rocks. Hadow appears to have slipped—although this is still only surmise—and to have knocked Croz from the position where he was standing firm. Their combined weight pulled Hudson from the rocks, and the combined weight of the three men pulled off Lord Francis Douglas.[17]

A doubtful pall crept over mountaineering, with some asking why such risky feats were undertaken, much as science had been casting doubt on the world of religious faith but a few years previous. But Whymper's tenacity, his swagger, his enthusiasm for the peaks made him a legend of that golden age. "For a whole segment of the only partially informed public," Clark wrote of Whymper in his later years, "Whymper *was* mountaineering for the rest of his life."[18] He was the prominent figure for many subsequent mountaineers who were driven to proceed into the unknown, some for conquest, others to make a pilgrimage towards greater understanding of the human condition.

During the closing years of that golden age of mountaineering, another Whymper, also an artist, adventurer, and engraver, was following a man in British Columbia, one Alfred Waddington, who had hired him for his services. During the year in which Edward Whymper was relentlessly pursuing success on the Matterhorn, his older brother Frederick set out on the sail-assisted steamship *Tynemouth* from the Thames, bound for Victoria, B.C.

"There was an adventurous instinct in the family," wrote Edward Whymper biographer F.S. Smythe. Their father, Josiah Wood Whymper, instead of becoming a brewer or seaman as other members of the family had, had decided to break away and follow his talents as an artist. Josiah "travelled to London with the few traditional shillings in his pocket," wrote Smythe, "carrying with him a pair of busts he had carved. He sold his busts, obtained work, and soon achieved fame and fortune both as a wood-engraver and an original artist." Although watercolour was his medium of choice, he set up a business that produced wood-engraved illustrations for books. Marrying Elizabeth Claridge soon after, Josiah had eleven children, the first to emerge being Frederick and Edward, who also "inherited his artistic tendencies, as well as an instinct for travel and adventure." Edward had a knack for the creative, and early in his teens "he was taken from school and apprenticed to his father's business." This skill was something Frederick would pursue as well, just in a different part of the world.[19]

As Frederick Whymper biographer Peter Johnson noted, "[Frederick] Whymper was trained as a woodblock engraver and illustrator, a skill that, for most of his lifetime, was the only means of adding illustration to a text."[20] Arriving in Victoria, British Columbia, in September 1862 after a three-month voyage, Whymper soon made connections via his excellent credentials. The winter bore fruit for his search for employment in the far reaches of the British Empire. "During the winter of 1862–63, Whymper's background as an artist brought him into contact with many of Victoria's professional elite," Johnson wrote. One person he encountered was George Wallace, "a correspondent with the *British Colonist*," who, through his tales of the struggling gold miners in the Cariboo, influenced Whymper to make a sketching trip north. He began his trip capturing the mountainous environment surrounding the settlement of Yale. He then went farther north and became very productive, sketching "the raw, topographic reality of British Columbia's frontier settlements." Bringing this imagery back to Victoria, he developed a market for his work. "For Victoria's colonial officials and the educated elite, he drew vistas that captured his idea of 'the sublime,' a notion first expressed by romantic poets at the beginning of the nineteenth century. Artists began to record pristine landscapes as a fresh source of transcendence beyond the Christian God. Whymper understood the need to 'let nature be your teacher,' and his art included elements that reflected the exultation of the human condition through communion with nature."[21]

It was not long before the work of Frederick Whymper caught the attention of Alfred Waddington. Whymper's sketches and watercolour paintings encouraged the entrepreneur in his scheme to build roadways and infrastructure to aid the struggling miners Whymper had heard about from Wallace. In 1864, "Alfred Waddington sought [Whymper] out to create sketches of the country from Bute Inlet across the coastal mountains to the Chilcotin Plateau," wrote biographer Johnson. Whymper would create the visuals that would encourage investment, showing the rough-hewn wilderness that Waddington had to contend with to build these roads, which would further encourage economic development in the new colony.

> Waddington's brainchild was to construct an alternate road to the Cariboo that would bypass the New Westminster-Harrison Lakes route to Lillooet and the proposed Fraser Canyon trail from Yale to Lytton

altogether. It would be shorter and less expensive than the planned American route from Portland, Oregon, through Washington to the BC interior. Waddington, like Whymper, knew that transportation costs alone on these routes made them impractical. Waddington's road would begin at the head of Bute Inlet and follow the Homathko River through the coast mountains to connect with the Fraser River at Fort Alexandria on the Chilcotin Plateau.[22]

A completed project, an attempt to overcome nature with science and engineering for the sake of economic prosperity, would give challenged miners a route out with their hauls of gold. The project would have a "deep-water townsite at the head of Bute Inlet" planned for receiving the incoming raw gold. Of course, Waddington's plan was to become rich off this scheme; he was an entrepreneur and a speculator, after all. Having liquidated many of his own assets to fund his plan, he would hire surveyor Robert Homfray to do the work of making the trail in, and architect Herman Tiedemann to "map the route and draw a townsite at the head of the inlet."[23] But 1863 had already seen many setbacks in the form of a severe snowmelt destroying a great deal of built roadway in B.C.'s interior, and the great expense of the overall scheme was causing Waddington some doubt over whether he should persevere. But persevere he did. When Whymper came in at this point in the project, his job description was straightforward. In the spring months of 1864, "Whymper's job was to produce favourable drawings and water-colours, which Waddington intended to send to the *Illustrated London News* in hopes of enticing even more unsuspecting lords of Fleet Street to put money into his venture."[24]

One of Frederick Whymper's images, "Great Glacier, Bute Inlet," which captures the glacier that would later feature architect Tiedemann's name and act as a guide for a mountaineer named Ferris Neave from Winnipeg to go after the tallest mountain in British Columbia, named after Whymper's employer, is also featured in Frederick Whymper's own book. First published in 1869 by John Murray of Albemarle Street in London, England, *Travel and Adventure in the Territory of*

Alaska, formerly Russian America—now ceded to the United States—and in various other parts of the North Pacific is something of a Boy's Own adventure illustrated with Whymper's engravings. "The opening chapters contain some earlier reminiscences of British Columbia and Vancouver Island," Whymper establishes in the preface.[25] Where the first chapter describes the voyage out from England, rounding Cape Horn to San Francisco, then to Victoria and the "Cariboo mines," Chapter 2 tells of "the Glaciers of Bute Inlet, British Columbia," a remote, forlorn place that was bound to impress and enthrall readers in faraway England. The geography of the coast and Coast Mountains had to be seen to be believed, Whymper wrote.

> A glance at the map of British Columbia shows us one of the most broken jagged coastlines in the world, with arms of the sea innumerable, into each of which some river, small or large, finds its way. These streams, fed by numerous tributaries, born of the snow and ice, pass through the valleys of the Cascade and coast ranges, bordering on the Gulf of Georgia, Straits of Fuca, and adjacent coast. The general character of these mountain ranges is Alpine; perpetual snow reigns in their upper regions, and glaciers exist in their valleys.[26]

Frederick Whymper

This is how Whymper introduces his readers to this fascinating land of superlatives, an alpine region of pristine beauty and unfamiliar coastlines. Whymper, of course, needed to illustrate for the reader the raison d'être for his journey by mentioning his employer. "A direct route from the coast into the Cariboo mines by the way of Bute Inlet had been projected and partially carried out in the year 1864; and in consequence the writer was induced to visit this otherwise inaccessible country. A schooner, with men and supplies on board, left

Victoria, on Vancouver Island, on the 16th March of that year; and he then took the opportunity, kindly given him by the projector of the road, Mr. Alfred Waddington, of paying the glaciers a visit."[27]

The schooner arrived at the mouth of Bute Inlet on March 22, and later on that day arrived at the mouth of the Homathko River. This was the traditional territory of the Homalco First Nation, and as Andrew Scott wrote in his update of Captain John T. Walbran's *British Columbia Coast Names*, *Homathko* could just be a way of presenting *Homalco*. "The name of the Homalco people, which has been spelled many different ways, can be translated as 'swift water,'" Scott wrote in his entry for *Homathko River*.

> Three traditional village sites were maintained by this Northern Coast Salish group, formerly known as the Mainland Comox, at the mouths of three major rivers (including the Homathko). Most tribal members now live at Sliammon, N of Powell R, or at Campbell R. The remote rugged valley of the 137-km Homathko River was considered as a possible railroad and wagon route into the BC Interior in the 19th century. The idea was abandoned after a crew of road builders was attacked and killed in 1864, an event that led to the so-called Chilcotin War.[28]

Frederick Whymper described a visit by "Chilcoten Indians" on board their schooner. "They had rings through their noses," Whymper wrote, "were much painted, and wore the inevitable blanket of the coast."[29] Once they started for the road, Whymper took note of the thick snowpack, the voracious mosquitoes, and the extraordinarily sized old-growth cedar and hemlock. Along the established road, following the river nearly all the way, Whymper greatly admired the "superb" views. "Purple cliffs rose—pine-clad and abrupt, whilst below the Homathco [*sic*] made its way to the sea," Whymper noted.[30] By April 19, they had gone as far as they could along the road before meeting up with the construction crew. Hiring a "Chilcoten" guide, they set out for the "Great Glacier." A venture into the woods was followed by their first glimpse of this exotic phenomenon after a rough journey during which "we found that rotten snow covered the ground, logs, and underbrush, to a depth of several feet, and travelling with the loads we carried were [*sic*] hardly pleasurable. We, however, pushed on, and, after following the Homathco River more or less closely for the greater part of a day, we reached the first glacier stream, and soon obtained a distant view of the great 'frozen torrent' itself, with the grand snow-peaks behind it."[31]

The guide Whymper had employed to get him that far was Tellot, for whom the glacier immediately north of Tiedemann Glacier is named.

Whymper explored the terminal moraines of the glacier, ruminating on an earlier time in which these massive ice structures were commonplace, and noting boulder-strewn surfaces, water pouring out from icy caves, and trees being torn from the land by the immeasurable force of the slowly sliding glacier. "The mountains behind were lofty, and one peak was slightly horned; whilst one immense black mass of rock, with precipitous sides, reared itself from the surrounding purity. After spending the day in such crude examination as my time would permit, I returned late in the evening to the camp, where Tellot had remained all

Frederick Whymper's wood-engraved illustration "Great Glacier, Bute Inlet."

23

day. From his manner, I should suppose that he thought me a fool for my pains, although he showed some little interest in my sketches."[32]

If he had not had a boat to catch to take him down Bute Inlet, the draw of the glaciers and views of the mountains beyond might have enticed Frederick Whymper to explore farther. All it would have required was time, determination, and tenacity—the kind of tenacity displayed by his younger brother Edward Whymper, perhaps, who spent climbing season after season returning to attempt the Matterhorn, and who would eventually reach the top of a peak deemed impossible to climb. This tenacity would later be seen in the 1920s and 1930s, when Don and Phyllis Munday pursued, climbing season after climbing season, the final spire of another peak far away in North America. That peak was Mystery Mountain, or as it would be named later, Mount Waddington. Begun on a summer's day in 1925 when the Mundays, a married couple whose passion was mountaineering, spotted a prominent peak on a climbing trip to Mount Arrowsmith, the quest, the pilgrimage to a new final spire, was on. The inner spirit had been kindled again.

CHAPTER 1:
EARLY ATTEMPTS

It was the far-off finger of destiny beckoning. It was a marker along the trail of adventure, a torch to set the imagination on fire.[1]

—Don Munday, *The Unknown Mountain*

I t was on their climb of Mount Arrowsmith in June of 1925 that Don and Phyllis Munday first spotted something of note.

The accomplished mountaineering couple, along with Thomas H. Ingram, had moved from their Cameron Lake camp towards Arrowsmith's peak, known to be just shy of 6,000 feet. They were hurried along by the less-than-ideal weather. Snowfall was obliterating what Don Munday called an "easy gradient," and rather than risk the snowfall locking them down in the available cabin at 4,200 feet, they decided to make the best of the existing conditions and climb to the peak.[2] "Thick weather continued until the top of the so-called first peak was reached," Munday later wrote, "but here a momentary glimpse of part of the mountain gave us partial bearings, sufficient to negotiate the wall of fine cliffs facing towards Arrowsmith."[3] This first peak was usually the turnaround point for most climbers, Munday knew, but his climbing party was determined to carry on. They were in need of a break, however, and their gamble paid off with visibility improving after the wait. "A wait of about an hour and a half on this peak was finally rewarded by a dramatic sweeping away of the clouds from Arrowsmith," he wrote, "the last to clear."[4] The fresh snow broke free of its moorings and avalanched at

Don Munday's 1928 sketch map of the Coast Range where "Mystery Mountain" was to be found.

Don Munday (left) and Tom Ingram (right) look east towards the Coast Range while on their 1925 Mount Arrowsmith climb.

every opportunity around them. But despite this, and frequent sinkings to the waist in the powder, the climbing party found holds in protruding rock. "The summit of the north peak was reached at 3 p.m."[5] The trio spent ninety minutes enjoying the view from that peak. The summit "overlooks the southern half of the Island, commands a view of the Pacific, the Strathcona Park mountains (7,000 feet), and about 200 miles of the Coast Range; in fact," Munday expressed approvingly, "the view is of surpassing interest and extent."[6]

It was the view of the Coast Range that gave them pause.

In 1928, in the *Canadian Alpine Journal*, Don Munday begins his article "Exploration in the Coast Range" with an acknowledgement of how mountaineers were initially brought to awareness of Mystery Mountain through the 1924 Geological Survey Summary Report. Noted by Dr. Victor Dolmage, the mountain's elevation was "over 13,000 feet in height."[7] As for the name of Mystery Mountain adopted early on by mountaineers, Munday wished to clarify that it "has been used here owing

to the wide currency it has gained, and also because the Geographic
Board of Canada has so far taken no action to transfer the suggested
name 'Mt. Waddington' from a peak near Yellowhead Pass."[8] The next
clarification, preceding Don's description of the Mundays' 1927 effort
to ascend Mystery Mountain, puts to rest how they came upon what
they saw to the east and their desire to climb this mysterious rock hidden in the clouds. The climb would become contagious because of its
mythical allure, thanks largely to the writing of Don Munday.

> My wife and I had long cherished a wish to explore the
> unknown heart of the Coast Range, but the wish first
> took definite form as the result of a trip to Mt. Arrow-
> smith, Vancouver Island, early in June, 1925. Persis-
> tent rain finally yielded us a few hours of crystal clarity
> in the wake of a heavy snowstorm on the heights. To
> the westward the Pacific Ocean, beyond the Alberni
> Canal, shimmered like pearl. Southward, cloud hid the
> Olympic Range in the State of Washington. To the
> northwest the glacial peaks of Strathcona Park were
> partly revealed. On the easterly side of Vancouver
> Island, above the violet expanse of Georgia Strait, the
> snowy Coast Range reared a gleaming rampart above a
> purple base, extending more than a hundred and fifty
> miles northwestward before fading in cloudy distance.
> Cloud-windrows still built mocking mountain forms
> upon a foundation of authentic peaks further inland.
>
> One massive rock peak almost due north seemed to
> dominate the distant horizon somewhat eastward of a
> line drawn to the head of Bute Inlet. As chiefly the
> summits near the coast were clear, it was concluded,
> wrongly, however that this peak was close to tidewa-
> ter. (Mystery Mountain lies approximately 30 miles
> further west, and was not seen on this occasion.) We
> resolved then and there to visit Bute Inlet to look for
> the mountain we had seen. T.H. Ingram was the other

Don and Phyllis Munday were the celebrated mountaineering couple of their day.

member of the first party. A.E. Augur [sic], formerly of Summerland, B.C. was added to the original Mt. Arrowsmith party.[9]

A few months later, under the editorship of H.D. Foster, *The B.C. Mountaineer* (the official publication of the British Columbia Mountaineering Club, published monthly) began to chronicle a sudden interest in the Coast Range by member Don Munday. Following a piece in the October 1925 issue about the Trip Committee's plans for winter excursions to local hills a few miles from Vancouver such as Capilano Peak, Dam Mountain, and Mount Strachan, Foster laid out how Don and Phyllis Munday, T.H. Ingram, and E.A. Agur took it upon themselves to explore the comparatively distant mountain range, which had garnered little interest previously in the pages of the newsletter, and "made a trip into the mountains at the head of Bute Inlet about one hundred and fifty miles from Vancouver."[10] The piece comprised four brief paragraphs introducing the difficult terrain, illustrating the challenging times for the foursome who had made the perilous journey north, and accentuating that "the trip was a most strenuous one, it being necessary to pack from the water's edge to the camping place at 5,500 feet, first through the dense coastal bush, and then over 3,000 feet of rockslide."[11]

These pains having been taken, further description makes it clear they were rewarded with extraordinary sights. "From the peak of Mount Rodney," Foster's piece continued, mentioning a peak just southeast of where the Homathko River pours into Bute Inlet, "which is about 8,000 feet, a sea of mountains could be seen stretching in a northeasterly direction to Chilco Lake about 40 miles distant. Mr. Munday states that the panorama from this peak is the finest he has ever seen."[12] This kind of praise, coming from the likes of the adventurous mountaineering couple Don and Phyllis Munday, was quite a testimonial. This statement was tempered with the further missive that "the district would not be practical for a Summer Camp," referring to the club's regular seasonal event through the Alpine Club of Canada, "there being no central point from which a number of climbs could be made." Could this statement have staved off the timid and enflamed the more adventurous of trampers of these hills? What is most notable in the brief piece

E. Athol Agur, Thomas H. Ingram, and Don and Phyllis Munday boarding the SS *Chelohsin* to travel up Bute Inlet and begin their explorations.

is not the exclamations of glorious vistas of the mountains of Bute Inlet, but the fact that not one mention of Mystery Mountain is made. Was this not the raison d'être for the reconnaissance trip in the first place?

"We just couldn't wait," said Phyllis Munday in a sound recording of January 1964 titled "Old Ways to Waddington." "So, in the middle of September, we went with Mr. Ingram and Athol Agur and took the Union boat to Orford Bay, the old *Chelohsin*."[13]

In *The Unknown Mountain*, first published in 1948, Don Munday chose to segue from their final night camping on the shores of Cameron Lake after their Mount Arrowsmith trip in June, to Don, Phyllis, Tom, and Athol on board the SS *Chelohsin* en route to Bute Inlet in September.[14] The *Chelohsin* was a Union steamship, built in Dublin, that arrived in Vancouver in late 1911, originally slated for northern runs. A twin-screw vessel, 1,134 gross tons with a steel hull, the ship had been given an ideal review from the captain who got her to Vancouver: "She was like a racing yacht." *Chelohsin* was eventually put on the logging camp routes, earning the nickname the *Logger's Hearse* from returning tree fallers who had met untimely accidents in the dangerous

SS *Chelohsin*, Bute Inlet, 1926.

profession; locals called her the *Charlie Olsen*. Her captain, Jack Edwards, "maintained his muscular physique by taking an axe into the nearby woods to chop trees during layovers in Powell River."[15]

During that 1925 voyage on the *Chelohsin*, at the entrance to Bute Inlet Don Munday noted their stop at Church House, a Homalco settlement. This was also known as New Church House, Old Church House having been a settlement on Sonora Island in which the people of Homalco First Nations had been placed by Catholic missionaries. New Church House offered good fishing and shelter from prevailing winds. "Church House is mainly an Indian settlement," Munday wrote, describing the scene from the bow of the steamship, moored at a log float thirty feet from a granite cliff, "the church being the largest building among a score of houses on natural terrace below a mountainside recently devasted by fire. The frame houses had been spaced with un-Indian order; in fact, the whole settlement and its population reflected the white man's attempt to mould an aboriginal people to civilized ways in one generation."[16]

First impressions as SS *Chelohsin* cruised up Bute Inlet were promising. "Several shapely mountains 4,000 to 6,000 feet high overlook the

Left to right: R.C. Johnson, Don Munday, Albert Munday, and Athol Agur, 1926.

threshold of Bute Inlet," Munday wrote, "but heights increase farther up the channel. After 20 miles we entered Orford Bay, at the mouth of a valley flanked by handsome glacial summits 7,000 or 8,000 feet high."[17] Ingram received a deep cut to his arm after a slip on the deck of the *Chelohsin*, and visiting a nearby logging camp's doctor was recommended. After proselytizing on how those from more genteel places romanticize the toughness of loggers, Munday writes of the head of a logging camp introducing him to Jack McPhee, "a tall, sparsely built, weather-beaten trapper who lived alone at the head of Bute Inlet, some 26 miles further on."[18] Agreeing to take the mountaineering party to Ward Point, McPhee suggested to them to make a climb of Mount Rodney to gauge the impressive mountain scenery the area had to offer.

After having achieved the top of Rodney, the Mundays, Ingram, and Agur could see a summit of a little over 9,000 feet that McPhee knew as The Castle; the climbing party renamed it Bute Mountain. The views to the north and east were sublime, with clouds obscuring clear views. Don Munday was not above speculating that they could see what their previous view from Mount Arrowsmith had hinted at. "East of Homathko valley and still about 40 miles distant loomed a massive rock dome," Munday wrote somewhat restrainedly, "which might be the one sighted from Mt. Arrowsmith."[19] They also speculated on the heights of the peaks they saw from this vantage point, estimating them at 11,000 to 12,000 feet: "The great pinnacle exceeded 13,000 feet!" Munday wrote in a giddy tone, as though having found the mother lode. "But who would believe us?"

Beyond learning much about the area around the head of the Homathko River, Phyllis Munday was also impressed with what the climbing party found from the higher altitude of Mount Rodney. "Part way up Rodney we got a very fine view looking up the valley," she later said during her "Old Ways to Waddington" presentation: "But we went to the top of the ridges here and climbed Mount Rodney and made the first ascent of Mount Blade. But the view up the Homathko valley was absolutely wonderful! We could see for about 30 miles up the valley to the great peak, which at that time had no name, and all its magnificent neighbours."[20]

This significant if brief bit of reconnaissance had merely whetted their appetites. They boarded the *Chelohsin* for the return voyage to Vancouver with a better understanding of the scope of the mountainous country they had viewed from the top of Rodney. "We had set out to find one imposing peak; perhaps we sighted it," Don Munday wrote self-deprecatingly, "but certainly we had found a whole range of mightier peaks, with one entitled to rank among the great mountains of Canada, and, possibly, not for its height alone."[21]

In 1948, Don Munday would dedicate his book *The Unknown Mountain* to his wife. This was notable; it was how he acknowledged his wife's abilities and accomplishments without seeming sentimental or obligated to do so by societal propriety. He was doing so out of admiration. In the initial chapter of the book, where Munday describes their September 1925 foray up Bute Inlet, he mentions the weight of their packs as being on average about forty-five pounds "but apportioned more or less according to our carrying ability—a few weeks before this Phyl unaided had carried a 110-pound girl part-way down Grouse Mountain in an emergency."[22] It is clear from Don's writing that he and "Phyl" had a connection beyond climbing.

During the off-season, the Mundays were developing more than their understanding of peaks in the Coast Mountains. They took part in a

B.C. Mountaineering Club photographic exhibition, in which entries were judged by members of the club and prizes were awarded to the photographers of top entries. In the category of Pictorial Photography, Don Munday took first prize. He also received second prize in the category of Wild Birds and Animals. But Phyllis Munday took home more prizes than her husband, winning first prize in both Geological Phenomena and Panorama categories. She won second prize in the categories of Trees and Flowers and won third prize in Group of Six Unenlarged. With their skills at visually documenting their adventures using the relatively recent technology of the still camera, this duo was becoming more than just a celebrity mountaineering couple. In a field dominated by men, however, Phyllis was standing out.

Although her husband was already a prolific writer whose work was beginning to be published in *The B.C. Mountaineer* and the *Canadian Alpine Journal* (*CAJ*), Phyllis had the distinction of being a female author of an article appearing in the 1924 *CAJ*. But it was the subject of the article that brought her into the limelight as a female mountaineer in a male-dominated sport: the first ascent made by a woman of Mount Robson, the tallest mountain in the Rockies, previously thought to be the tallest mountain in British Columbia.[23]

In Phyllis Munday's article, she tells her version of the climb made at the 1924 Alpine Club of Canada–sponsored annual summer camp, which B.C. Mountaineering Club members were attending from Vancouver. It was a well-attended event in Mount Robson Provincial Park, and Don and Phyl Munday signed up for several climbs, including an attempt on Mount Robson. The climb had not been attempted since the first ascent during the Alpine Club of Canada camp in 1913 and would be guided by the legendary Conrad Kain, who had guided that first summit. As Munday biographer Kathryn Bridge noted, this was a first for the emerging mountaineering couple.

> The 1924 camp had been selected by ACC President A.O. Wheeler to enable a second attempt by club members, and he had hired Kain to once more guide members on the summit quest. It would be Wheeler who would decide, based upon all the names on the

sign-up sheet, how many parties would make the attempt, and who would be selected. Don and Phyl, and presumably Bev Cayley and other BCMC members (who were, like Don and Phyl, also Alpine Club members) signed up. It was worth the shot, they all thought, although being from the west coast, and new to ACC camps (it was the Mundays' first), their mountaineering skills and credentials were little known by Wheeler and others in the ACC Executive.[24]

The first paragraph of Phyllis Munday's *CAJ* article notes how the climbs in which women were permitted to participate usually did not include technical high-altitude climbs, so Phyl's inclusion on the Robson ascent came as a shock to her. It followed soon after their ascent of Mount Mumm. "The return from a climb is hardly the time one expects a grand surprise. This was my experience from returning from Mt. Mumm, when Mr. Wheeler told my husband to be prepared to go to the high camp on Mt. Robson next morning and, in spite of the prevailing impression that no women would be allowed to attempt the 'big climb,' I found I was to go also."[25]

The mountaineering couple would be in the second climbing party to attempt Robson at the 1924 camp. The Mundays would be in the company of Andy Drinnan and Fred Lambart (who would be deputy leader the following year on the first ascent of the tallest peak in Canada, Mount Logan). "Shortly before starting," Phyllis added, "we found our number increased by A.E. Buck and Mr. Porter[.] Joe Saladana, a guide employed by Donald Phillips, completed the party."[26]

Despite the ascent being dangerous, and "Conrad's running fire of excruciatingly funny anecdotes sometimes threatened to interfere with our showing as climbers," coolness prevailed and they made it to the top. Phyllis described the final steps towards their famous guide and the summit with enthusiasm. "'Conrad's on top, thank heaven!' I thought, for he was gathering my slack fast. As I stepped up beside him he held my rope and said in a very satisfying tone, 'There! Lady! you are the first woman on the top of Mt. Robson.' I said out loud 'Thank Heaven!' For it was a four-year ambition at last achieved."[27]

Club members who made the ascent of Mt. Robson in 1924, including Don Munday (bottom row, second from left) and Phyllis Munday (bottom row, third from left).

But in 1926, the ambition of Phyl and her husband Don was to find out more about the mystery mountain that was out there in the Coast Range. In the July 1926 edition of *The B.C. Mountaineer*, now under the editorship of Neal M. Carter (who would also figure into the lore of the mystery mountain in later years), a brief but tantalizing paragraph indicated what was to come in the next issue. "Although unsuccessful in attaining the summit of the high peak which formed the object of a five-weeks' trip to the country west of Chilko Lake, Mr. and Mrs. Don Munday and party have returned with much interesting information regarding the wonderfully-glaciated area surrounding this peak. The full report of this expedition is anticipated with greatest pleasure."[28]

Once the climbing season of 1925 came to a close, the prize spotted from Mount Rodney obsessed the mountaineering couple. "Throughout the winter and spring Phyl and I were planning to try to reach 'Mystery Mountain'—as the people of British Columbia soon came to call the great unknown peak—in the summer of 1926."[29] From their vantage point on Rodney, it appeared that the "logical route by which to explore the

Trapper Jack McPhee (left) with fellow wolf hunter Ed Atkins (right).

unknown range seemed to be to follow the Homathko valley for about 30 miles."[30] Despite "squally weather," the Mundays returned to Bute Inlet in the second week of May.[31] With the ideal route to Mystery Mountain perceived then as travelling the Homathko River, the couple were on a hunt for reconnaissance about the Homathko Valley. With the help of Lee Hand, "one of the principals of a logging company starting to log along Teaquahan River (Eva Creek), just east of the mouth of the Homathko," the Mundays had their fifteen-foot rowboat with a small engine towed into position. Jack McPhee was once again part of this enterprise as "he insisted that we make his cabin our headquarters. … Nailed to the cabin wall," Don Munday wrote later, describing the interior decor of McPhee's cabin, "were paws of a fair-sized grizzly bear which McPhee said had been shot almost from his cabin door." The cabin "reeked with stale bear-fat from a big hide drying on a frame indoors."[32]

McPhee was the Mundays' guide up the Homathko as the couple took notes of the hazards along the way. Don Munday noted the glacial activity of millennia, especially of Mount Evans, where "the whole western face had been planed smooth by ice up to an elevation of 5,000 feet or more."[33] Where the river's tidal activities were concerned, the Mun-

Handlogger and trapper August Schnarr hauled a floathouse up above the waterline, where he and his wife raised three children.

August Schnarr with an impressive catch of trout from the Homathko River.

One of August Schnarr's cabins in the Bute Inlet area, where the Mundays stayed during their reconnaissance and expeditions.

days hoped the summer would have a forgiving freshet for when it was time to make their way up. "Clouds hid all the higher summits," the couple noted, "but we glimpsed part of Waddington Glacier, which was the big one seen from Mt. Rodney." They were beginning to piece together the country they had seen from the peak, making note of landmarks and giving them names such as Pitchfork Gap, a place where the main current of the Homathko forced its way through a large logjam.

The next day's ascent of a shoulder of Mount Evans was aborted due to significant cloud cover. But the day after that, they followed McPhee to a place called Superb Bay and met handlogger and trapper August Schnarr. The Mundays saw that Schnarr had created a comfortable home for his family, having hauled a floathouse up on the shore beyond where the water could reach it. "We found Schnarr's three chubby children playing on the beach bare-footed and thinly clad, but with no show of discomfort on this raw day. In later days these girls reared a cougar[34] for a pet."[35]

Querying Schnarr about the river they intended to follow to get to Mystery Mountain, the Mundays discovered he knew much about trapping but little about the tributary valleys about which they sought information. In fact, it looked as though the Mundays already knew more than Schnarr from their observations from Mount Rodney. The information of most use from Schnarr was about successful river travel; he insisted that the river was behaving unusually that spring and told them what to look out for.[36]

The following morning saw them "under wintry-looking skies" on board the SS *Chelohsin* for the return to Vancouver. They were as ready as they could be for the season's attempt.

The B.C. Mountaineer reported in June 1926 that

> Mr. and Mrs. Don Munday, supported by Mr. T.H. Ingram and others, are emulating the success which crowned the efforts to conquer Canada's highest peak, Mt. Logan, by making an expedition to what may prove "the highest point in all this province." Considering the fact that part of the summit of Mt. Fairweather, 15,400 feet, lies in this province, this new "mystery mountain" must indeed be a giant.

Left to right: R.C. "Johnnie" Johnson, E. Athol Agur, Thomas H. Ingram, Albert Munday, Phyllis Munday, and Don Munday on the SS *Chelohsin*.

43

It was first seen by Mr. and Mrs. Munday from Mt. Arrowsmith, and later from a summit above the head of Bute Inlet, last year. Apparently lying in the unmapped district surrounding Chilco Lake, its inaccessibility will probably cause the party to be gone a month.[37]

Events seemed to have snowballed via the excitement generated through print media; in fact, Don and Phyllis Munday had not entirely seen Mystery Mountain from Mount Arrowsmith, merely the hint of it; they saw more of the mass from Mount Rodney.

"Several days later they were home and packing supplies," wrote Munday biographer Kathryn Bridge about their brief stop after their reconnaissance trip. "On May 22, an advance party of Don and R.C. Johnny [sic] Johnson left Vancouver with most of the equipment and food required for the expedition."[38]

Readers of *The B.C. Mountaineer* used to day-trip descriptions and meeting reports must have been impressed with what appeared in the August 1926 issue. Don Munday penned an article revealing what had been alluded to in the brief paragraph in the previous issue. It was clear now that he and his climbing party were prioritizing "an approach to the monarch of the range." The article began, "Information furnished by the Geological Survey and borne out by views obtained from Mt. Rodney, Bute Inlet, led Mr. and Mrs. W.A.D. Munday, Mr. T.H. Ingram, A.E. [sic] Agur, A.R. Munday and R.C. Johnson to make a five-weeks' trip up the Homathko River to the mountain which work of Dominion and Provincial surveyors indicates is over 13,000 feet high."[39]

This must have fired up the imaginations of readers of the newsletter, as previously it was Mount Robson, measured at just under 13,000 feet high and recently scaled in 1924 by the Mundays, that was the tallest peak of the Rockies and thought to be the highest peak in British Columbia. There was now a new objective to which the mountaineers of B.C., not yet out of the year's climbing season, could aspire.

"The party left May 29 and returned July 5," Munday wrote. He likely submitted this article with haste to editor Neal Carter, who must have realized he had a scoop on his hands. Adventure into the unknown was *de rigueur* for mountaineers born of a European tradition. They were

Don Munday pulls Athol Agur up difficult terrain in the Bute Inlet area with a rope in 1926.

seeking new sources for expeditions that might rival those of the Matter-horn, the Rockies, and, most prominent in the minds of those following global mountaineering efforts, the three recent attempts on the tallest peak in the world, Everest.

The article goes on to tell of an adventure that involved dangerous water travel in a boat powered only by an outboard motor, backpacking through difficult terrain, and hauling equipment and supplies by relay. It indicated challenging terrain and waterways in which the expedition's canoe was punctured twice, almost losing much of the climbers' neces-sary gear. "Cloudy, unsettled weather prevailed throughout most of the trip and particularly baffled the party in finding a route across the inter-vening range of mountains, which exceed 10,000 feet in height."[40] Had this intrepid group of adventurers come across a range that rivalled that of the Rockies? The Alps? The Himalayas?

The hike along the Homathko River involved the crossing of several creeks. This required some innovative engineering and teamwork in order to be successful. Phyllis Munday remembered, in her oral presentation "Old Ways to Waddington," just how much had to be coordinated for

Don Munday makes a rope into a handrail, pulling it taut as Phyllis Munday crosses Scar Creek.

the successful crossing of these various tributaries, including one tricky one called Scar Creek.

> Athol Agur . . . had found a log projecting out over one of the channels and we ran a big log out onto it and then he jumped on to the other shore and we made the bridge firm by building a tower of rocks on the opposite side . . . with the wild creek absolutely shaking the thing almost to pieces on one end. Which was particularly disconcerting when you were carrying 60 pounds over it. However, we fastened the climbing rope on a tree on one shore and Don acted as the post on the other, and he kept the rope nice and tight, which made a very good handrail.[41]

Don Munday pointed out that the temptation to climb the nearby peaks was tantalizing, but they needed to stick to their plan: to find a route to the elusive mountain that was nestled among all of this grandeur, tucked in among extraordinary glaciers. "The big glacier of the region," Munday revealed, "probably covers not less than 80 miles." The revelations continued with his description of the "Coula Glacier" covering

The Munday party viewing Mount Waddington, 1926.

possibly thirty square miles. "Teidemann [*sic*] Glacier is about 10 miles long and possibly covers nearly 25 miles."[42]

In "Old Ways to Waddington," Phyllis Munday recalled a great moment for the entire party: their first close view of the mountain of mystery itself.

> We travelled up a little glacier, which was Bert Glacier (we nicknamed it) through a little pass onto the upper reaches of Waddington Glacier, and there we had our first view of Mount Waddington . . . it looked very forbidding and far away with all the icefalls in front of it. And the little peak, at least it looks little by comparison to all the rest, but it is the main tower of Waddington. I remember as we stood on the pass there looking at it all so excited and thrilled at the sight of finding the mountain we'd looked for. Mr. Ingram said: "What? That little thing? We'll be up there by noon." But it was several years before anybody climbed it.[43]

It wasn't just the size or length of these glaciers that Don Munday was trying to impress upon his readers, but the number of them. "Even

Members of the Munday climbing party in 1926.

on the 8,000 feet range to the south," Munday wrote, "there are glaciers with eight and nine tributaries each and descending to about 2,000 feet above sea level."[44] Could these glaciers allow for a direct route to the monumental mystery mountain they sought?

> The barrier range was crossed by a 9,000-foot pass in a 32-hour trip which carried the party to an elevation of approximately 10,000 feet. Regular readings of a barometer at the head of Bute Inlet were used as a check against the aneroid and the hysometer carried on the trip. The conclusion was reached that the mountain was 13,000 feet high. The route [eventually] attempted was found to involve the traverse of an 11,000-foot peak with little prospect of a way up the slim final pinnacle of the big peak.[45]

In the pages of *The B.C. Mountaineer*, this is the first mention of this final obstacle, a potentially unattainable goal that put doubt in the minds of even the Mundays. Could anything be more difficult than an ascent of Mount Robson? Was it possible this seemingly indefatigable mountaineering couple of the day, despite the fact that the expedition had "excellent" weather "and visibility of the best," could be deterred from their latest goal?

The new goal had been identified, but not named. What were mountaineers to call this new objective? "The Geological Survey favors the name 'Mt. George Dawson' after the eminent geologist who did his first work on the upper Homathko River," Munday concluded, leaving no explicit indications of his further ambitions or exploits in the area, but hinting that this was not to be the last foray by him and his wife or anyone else. However, he did indicate a metric for future expeditions into the Coast Range, should the objective be the attainment of this new summit. "Owing to the almost incredible network of glaciers surrounding the big peak," Munday wrote, "any future expeditions would have to be Mt. Logan expeditions on a smaller scale." He was referring to the 1925 adventure that had not only been a logistical boondoggle but had almost spelled doom for the expedition members.[46]

There is no clear point when the tale of the mountain of mystery went beyond British Columbia's mountaineering community and captured the attention of the Canadian mountaineering community. But a brief blurb in *The B.C. Mountaineer* in April 1927 indicates that Don Munday's photography had caught the eye of the Alpine Club of Canada, and specifically the *Canadian Alpine Journal*: "We regret to learn and announce the lecture promised us by Don Munday had to be deferred for some time, as his slides had to be in Winnipeg by a certain date that did not allow us time to arrange a showing, but we hope to have the entertainment later."[47]

The postponement of Don Munday's lecture must have been disappointing to Vancouver members of the B.C. Mountaineering Club. But the title of this tiny paragraph tucked into the pages of the newsletter is significant: "Lecture on Mystery Mountain" seems to assume that Mystery Mountain already was known to its readers.

Don Munday considered the greatest finding of the 1926 expedition to have very little to do with route discovery or meteorological information or geology, but with the flow of glacier melt out to the sea. "The most important achievement of the 1926 expedition to Mystery Mountain," Munday wrote in the December 1927 issue of *The B.C. Mountaineer*, "was the discovery that Mystery Glacier was the source of the Franklin river, draining to Knight Inlet."[48] Later, in *The Unknown Mountain*,

Phyllis Munday making a meal at base camp, Waddington expedition, 1926.

Munday wrote that the route of the 1926 expedition had proved "prohibitively difficult." He added that while 20/20 hindsight was beneficial, a better alternative had not presented itself. "Presumably," Munday continued, echoing what he had written in *The B.C. Mountaineer*, "the great southern glacier of the region drained to the Pacific Ocean at Knight Inlet by way of the Franklin River." He was favouring a western approach by water. Little by little, more was being learned about the terrain surrounding the mountain and what gear was appropriate to outwit the daunting environment. Don Munday's news in *The B.C. Mountaineer* also gave the keen reader a description of the forbidding landscape, above where any vegetation grew. "The mountain stands in an area of 400 square miles devoid of even scrub timber," Munday added, illustrating the lack of available firewood, "making it impossible to establish a base camp within striking distance of the mountain." Munday also highlighted the importance of windproof clothing, as the chill winds blowing down the glacier were a constant presence, and the necessary use of crampons because of the rugged conditions and the thawing of glacial ice at the snout.

Munday knew his readership: groups that perhaps had seen the more southerly peaks of the Coast Range, where club members might enjoy a day's climbing from a comfortable camp to reach their objective. "Climbers acquainted only with the friendly southern portion of the Coast Range," he wrote, inching his adventurous readers further to the edge of allure, "will find it hard to imagine the austere character of the region inland from Knight and Bute inlets where glaciers 10 miles in length are commonplace, and the peaks exceed in average difficulty the finest section of the Selkirks, while much of the region equals that range in average elevation—the Mystery Mountain area exceeds in height any equal area in the Selkirks."[49]

The Selkirks were a range foundational to mountaineering exploits in Canada. Cofounder of the Alpine Club of Canada and honorary president Arthur O. Wheeler wrote in 1928 in the *Canadian Alpine Journal*:

> Completion of the railway through the Selkirks in 1885
> led to the coming of mountaineers, explorers and lov-
> ers of nature. The following year, 1886, Glacier House,
> a pretty little chalet nestling in the forest at the base of

> Mt. Abbott, and facing a fine cascade falling 1,100 ft. from the slopes of Eagle Peak directly opposite, was built by the Railway Company. It was right beside the track and was built with the object of "feeding the trains," for the palatial dining car had not then been introduced. It soon became apparent that this beautiful spot, apart from the train service, would be a favourite with mountain climbers and votaries of the great out-of-doors.[50]

In this way, Wheeler not only made the Selkirks important to mountaineering in Canada, but also to Canadian nationalism, aligning them with the transnational railway.

Munday was also developing the forbidding reputation of Mystery Mountain, generating awe in readers but also throwing down the gauntlet, creating a romanticism and allure for this remote environment, inhospitable to all but the hardiest of regional mountaineers, and also piquing the interest of those who might come from farther afield than British Columbia.

As Don M. Woods later wrote in the *CAJ*, further along in the history of attempts on Mount Waddington, Munday would be instrumental in developing the mountain's international appeal for climbers. "Since the discovery of Mt. Waddington from Vancouver Island in 1925 by Don and Phyllis Munday," Woods wrote, "this peak has become of foremost rank of mountaineers of both Canada and the United States."[51]

Munday's writing also highlighted the battle imagery that he and other mountaineer-writers of the time were developing in this interwar period. "All probable routes to the summit of Mystery Mountain are guarded," wrote Munday, treating the final peak as a bastion, or perhaps alluding to a prisoner of war constantly being watched, "by hanging glaciers, icefalls or rock towers ranging from gendarmes to individual mountains in size."[52]

The 1926 expedition had proved challenging, but the battle imagery portrayed in Don Munday's writing certainly didn't point to a retreat, but to an advance. The 1927 climbing season beckoned with further explorations to be made and, in the military mountaineering jargon of the time, perhaps a conquering. But there would be one casualty that would take the Mundays aback—and take away a brother-in-arms.

CHAPTER 2:

THE MONARCH OF THE COAST RANGE

There was something subduing in the influence of that silent and solemn and awful presence; one seemed to meet the immutable, the indestructible, the eternal, face to face, and to feel the trivial and fleeting nature of his own existence the more sharply by the contrast. One had the sense of being under the brooding contemplation of a spirit, not an inert mass of rocks and ice, —a spirit which had looked down, through the slow drift of the ages, upon a million vanished races of men, and judged them; and would judge a million more, —and still be there, watching, unchanged and unchangeable, after all life should be gone and the earth have become a vacant desolation.[1]

—Mark Twain, on the sight of "the mighty dome of the Jungfrau," *A Tramp Abroad*

On February 19, 1927, E. Athol Agur died in an avalanche in Vancouver's North Shore mountains. The March 1927 issue of *The B.C. Mountaineer* offered the following notice: "It was with the deepest regret that we heard on Saturday, February 19th, of the death of Mr. E.A. Agur, who was so closely associated with Don and Mrs. Munday in their attempt on the Mystery Peak."[2] His death left a gap in the climbing personnel for the Mundays' anticipated further attempt in 1927 to scale the monarch of the Coast Range, and they had also lost a friend and colleague.

A new trail had been created by the Grouse Mountain Resort Company that led to Kennedy Lake. "It appears that Mr. Agur and his partner, Mr. Johnston [*sic*], had just left their cabin on Little Goat and were following the new trail," reported *The B.C. Mountaineer*, "… and from the nature of the slide it would appear that it was started by themselves." The chance of an event of great magnitude had been increased by the ideal sunny conditions of several days and a fresh snowfall. "The hard crust, resulting from eight days of sunshine previously, coupled with a fresh fall of snow of about two feet and a rise in temperature, made conditions ripe for avalanches, and their combined weights precipitated this one."[3]

The "Johnston" mentioned in the article was none other than R.C. "Johnnie" Johnson. He survived the avalanche and struggled to the Grouse Mountain chalet for help, but despite the search that followed, Agur was not found and was presumed buried under the snow. Don Munday, in *The Unknown Mountain*, reflected upon the terrible event and how his friend Johnson had survived. "Johnnie's foot providentially hooked in the branches of a tough little cypress on the edge of the cliff. He hung there head down till the snow poured past, then climbed back. The slide went on down 800 feet to the shore of Kennedy Lake, taking Athol with it."[4]

The Mundays, along with BCMC members, thoroughly searched the gully into which Agur had fallen, but sadly, they were not successful in finding him.

> It was with sad hearts that the members of this club and the Alpine Club of Canada abandoned the search, realizing that Agur's body must be buried deep under tons of wet snow, and that it would be impossible to find him until the spring or summer thaws melted away the top covering.

> Mr. and Mrs. Munday have sent to the members of this Club who assisted in the search a note of appreciation, which we are quoting below:

> "Mrs. Munday and I wish to express our very deep appreciation of the efforts of members of the B.C. Mountaineering Club in the search for our friend, Mr. E.A. Agur, who perished almost within sight of his mountain home. We feel that the Club's rapidly growing record of unselfish response to such emergencies is creating an ideal of service in keeping with the finest mountaineering traditions, and one that future members of the Club will regard as one of their proudest heritages."[5]

Agur's body was indeed retrieved at the end of July.

Although this event was saddening for the Mystery Mountain climbers, the resolve built into the Mundays' message was characteristic of them. Agur's name would later be lent to a glacier and peak in the Coast

Range, not far from the Mystery Mountain he didn't get the chance to scale.

These difficult times were perhaps exacerbated by the Mundays' feeling that they were not much further ahead in finding the best route to the new peak. The trail they had tramped in 1926 was "prohibitively difficult." Don Munday was still writing about finding the right glacier that would guide them north. "Presumably the great southern glacier of the region drained to the Pacific Ocean at Knight Inlet by way of the Franklin River," Munday surmised. "Further exploration was therefore a necessary preliminary to the 1927 expedition."[6]

Phyllis Munday, in her 1964 retrospective recounting of the tale of the 1926 expedition in "Old Ways to Waddington," spoke about what she believed was the most revelatory part of the entire expedition. "Our most exciting part, in some ways, was perhaps the view down the Franklin Glacier. We didn't know its name at that time. But it was a great big glacier reaching off to the coast ... the great thing about that scene to us was we knew we would be able to come up the glacier and the valley looked particularly short from there to tidewater, and there were no deep valleys coming in, meaning that there were no big glacier creeks to worry us in future years."[7]

The mountain of mystery also had an official height now: 13,260 feet (since changed to 13,186 feet). The Mundays efforts were squarely prioritized in the 1928 *Canadian Alpine Journal*, taking top billing over articles by the likes of J.W.A. Hickson and his "Ascents in the Canadian Rockies" and J. Munroe Thorington's "A Mountaineering Journey through Jasper Park." The Coast Range had now pushed aside the allure of the Rockies and was becoming the focus of national climbing efforts, mountaineering interests, and armchair adventurers across Canada. Don and Phyllis Munday were gaining notoriety.

"Leaving Vancouver on the Union steamer 'Venture' on May 30," Don Munday wrote about the preliminary trip of 1927, "my wife and I arrived at Knight Inlet cannery at 10:30 p.m. the next day."[8] Munday noted with admiration the transportation juggernaut along the British Columbia coast. "What the passing of the one daily passenger train used to be years ago in prairie hamlets the arrival of the weekly coastal steamer is to these isolated settlements," he wrote approvingly, "but seven times intensified."[9] Munday's "Knight Inlet cannery" would sometimes later be referred to as the Glendale Cannery, and would prove to be a key stopping-off point in the expeditions to come. The Mundays navigated their way eight miles up Knight Inlet using an outboard motor, and they must have been vulnerable as their small, fifteen-foot craft was hit by Queen Charlotte Sound's west wind. At Kwalate Bay they encountered trapper Jim Stanton and his wife. Don Munday noted that

> he is typical of the hardy resourceful folk scattered along British Columbia's mountainous coast.[10] He gave us much useful information about Knight Inlet and advised us to go up the Klinakline valley by way of his trap-line and try to reach the Franklin Valley by climbing over the intervening ridge. Their hospitality, and the fact that we could not get into the mouth of the Klinakline (Kleenakleen) River before the next day's afternoon tide, decided us to spend the night with them.[11]

What is notable about the start of this introductory article to the Mountaineering Section of the *Canadian Alpine Journal*, and indicative of the changing political stance within the Alpine Club of Canada regarding this remote range in the far west, is the rapid decisions made in naming the geographical features of the region. "Since this article was written the Geographic Board of Canada has changed the name of Mystery Mountain or as was suggested Mount George Dawson to *Mount Waddington*. McCallum Mountain is *Devereux Mt.*, Trapper Creek is *Brew Creek*, Mt. Marcus Smith is *Mt. Marcus*, Mystery Glacier is *Franklin Glacier*, Gorge Creek is *Whitemantle Creek*, Mussel Creek, and Lake Laurette are *Devereux Creek* and *Lake*; Mt. Massive is *Mt. Reliance*."[12]

Many of these features had been temporarily named for practical reasons, merely to get a geographic fix in unexplored territory—such as McCallum Mountain, named after Phyl's sister and the Mundays' climbing companion during the 1927 expedition—and it was to be expected that those in power would throw their weight into the ring. Features such as Franklin Glacier, named by the Geographic Board of Canada "after Benjamin Franklin who in 1892 explored Tatla Lake down the Klinakline valley hoping to find a route to drive his cattle to the coast," would be frequently mentioned in the Mundays' accounts of their own explorations. In 1927, the Mundays had great hopes that Franklin Glacier would be the trail to the successful first ascent of the newly named Mount Waddington.

Don Munday's writing about First Nations history indicated that he and Phyllis were factoring it into the furtherance of their understanding of the Coast Range. "Indian tradition asserts that a village at Kwalate Bay was destroyed by a tidal wave caused by a landslide from the precipice of Adeane Point three miles away diagonally across the inlet," Munday wrote in the *Canadian Alpine Journal*.[13] This past tidal activity was corroborated by the Stantons, who had seen and experienced similar but much smaller waves caused by falling rock two miles across the bay from their home and the old Homalco village site.

The Mundays were sheltered by a cabin next to a channel of the Klinakline River and proceeded to a place they called Interior Valley, their introduction to an area that had been shaped from intense glacial activity over millennia. Making a short climb to the east, they found a vantage point from which they could gaze down upon Mystery Glacier (the soon-to-be-named Franklin Glacier), and they realized that the Stantons' advice had led them astray. "We had been misled, for the Franklin Valley was the logical approach. All the big peaks at the head of the glacier were in cloud. But we had cleared up some doubts as to the relationship of various topographical features, so the time was not wholly wasted."[14]

The Mundays noted the Franklin River Valley's nature as "a typical glacial gorge." The weather was erratic, and the couple agreed that upon their return to the area, under the burden of heavy packs, the thick vegetation would present a tiring and time-consuming problem. So they "set to work to cut a trail through to the glacier, about six miles in a straight line."[15] This degree of initiative on the part of the Mundays was admirable, as they spent several days cutting the trail. "At midday on June 13 we started down the inlet," Don wrote, "now oily calm."[16] Travelling in their skiff with the temperamental "kicker" (outboard motor) propelling them to Kwalate Bay, the couple was soon covered in ocean spray and looking forward to an evening in the company of the Stantons. The next day, they went on to Glendale Cannery, then onto the SS *Venture*.

A month later on July 18, Phyl and Don Munday were accompanied by Phyl's sister, Mrs. E.M. (Betty) McCallum, as they headed north on the *Venture*. The 1927 Mystery Mountain expedition had begun in earnest. They would discover whether the Franklin Glacier would be the highway of their hopes.

Don Munday noted that the glacier was not what it used to be. Despite its impressive length in 1927, he concluded that it had pulled back. "The glacier has retreated about a mile in the past 100 years," he wrote in the *Canadian Alpine Journal*.

> The old lateral moraines stand 500 feet above the river and indicate periods when the ice melted back slowly for some time before extensive losses took place again. The river had undermined the west margin of the glacier for about 400 yards so that it flowed through a defile between the 100-foot ice cliff and the dangerously unstable lateral moraine. The cavern of exquisite violet and blue from which the river emerged in July and August was about 150 feet in width; in June the cave did not exist; in September it was breaking down.[17]

It wasn't just that the glacier showed evidence of retreating in the recent past, but that it also failed to measure up to the Mundays' hopes. "The glacier proved disappointing as a highway," Don wrote. "It has a complex flow and descends in a series of steps, ice-fall conditions being hardly smoothed out before another break occurs."[18] Crevasses were a consideration, with the Mundays putting their crampons to use in the inconsistent and uncertain environment. "Crevasses on the westerly branch of Franklin Glacier forced a tediously indirect course as far a snow-line," Don Munday later wrote in *The Unknown Mountain*. The collapses into the snow were frightening, but they were also included as moments of climbing humour, in retrospect. "My leg sank full-length into a crevasse as I stopped to pick up an insect for Phyl's collection. Betty, who handled the rope with great skill, braced herself in case I broke through farther, but Phyl came forward from the rear and took the insect to stow away without a word as to my safety. Betty berated her for callousness, and tugged nobly on the rope."[19]

Don Munday is dwarfed among the séracs of the Franklin Glacier.

The scope of their environment never ceased to amaze them. Despite the shifty character of Franklin Glacier, the Mundays were collecting impressions not only of its vastness, but of the ancient times from which such a structure was born. "This vigorous river of ice must be a stubborn remnant of the last Ice Age," Don surmised, "and this region must have been one of the foci from which the vast continental ice sheet developed inland and towards the sea."[20]

The expedition members began naming features. This was for orientation's sake and also with future expeditions in mind. After a period of transporting supplies, Don Munday began working on mapping the area they were in. These efforts would culminate in a series of hand-drawn maps, one of which would appear alongside the article "The Apex of the Coast Range" in the *Canadian Alpine Journal* of 1928. Marvel Ridge was a raised point just behind their camp on August 4. From there they spotted Icefall Point just opposite a place Munday referred to on his map as the main icefall, where Franklin Glacier extended farther north, "the westerly branch passing from sight to unknown country, while the easterly branch, 'Corridor Glacier,' stretched back several miles towards the mouth of Ice Valley down which we had come from Waddington Glacier the previous year."[21] Confederation Glacier was like a tributary of the Franklin Glacier, "with four arms curving out of hidden valleys to form a trunk with three broad medial moraines sweeping down in fine curves."[22] However, it was the overbearing presence of the main pinnacle that was still the most striking, in this ice valley of superlatives. While still in awe at the sight of it, the adventuring trio were also planning how they might close in on the top of this shaft rising into the crisp-aired heavens.

> Of course, "Mystery Mountain's" unchallenged supremacy formed the dominating feature of a panorama worthy of attention in every direction. We saw the mountain revealed as less simple and compact in structure than we had supposed, but at this distance some details quite important to us remained unsuggested.

> From Mt. Munday to "Mt. Bell," which is the highest summit westward of "Mystery Mountain," the only real break in the range showed at the base of the long northwesterly ridge of "Mystery Mountain." To this we presently gave the name "Fury Gap."

> For climbing purposes a subsidiary ridge of the northwest ridge seemed to promise us a practicable route to reach the main mass of the mountain at about 12,000 feet.[23]

With a nod of admiration and love towards his wife Phyl, Munday wrote, "One student of life on snowfields and glaciers says ice-worms are most active during the heat of the day."[24] She had an interest in entomology and collected insects on their mountaineering expeditions. It seems difficult to believe that life could thrive in such an inhospitable environment, but iceworms seemed to enjoy this place, where they fed on snow algae.

Don Munday and Betty McCallum rest and admire a massive ice wall at Regal Glacier near Fury Gap during their 1927 Waddington expedition.

On Franklin Glacier we found them most numerous
and active just when evening began to chill the surface.
They were about an inch long and almost blackish in
colour. Their ability to squeeze between ice-crystals
doubtless accounts for Alaskan tales that ice-worms bore
through the ice. They seem at home in air or water,
often remaining deep in a pool, clinging to the icy wall
indefinitely. It has been supposed their food is algae of
the group to which "red snow" belongs, but of which it
is not the most common form.[25]

A scientist who may have held sway with mountaineers in British
Columbia was G.H. Wailes, one of whose articles was excerpted in *The
B.C. Mountaineer*. In it, he encouraged members of the mountaineering
community to assist the scientific community in furthering an understanding of cryoplankton. In the developing natural history section of
The B.C. Mountaineer, the following quote appears, which may have
underscored Phyl Munday's entomological interest:

The flora and fauna of the snow-fields and glaciers are
sometimes called collectively Cryoplankton; the flora
comprised in it numbers over seventy species recorded
from different parts of the globe but few specific iden-
tifications have been made in British Columbia.

Mountaineers could assist greatly in the investigation
of this interesting subject by sending samples of any
Cryoplankton they may find, as soon after collection is
practicable, to the curator of the Vancouver City Museum.
Mr. Menzies, if applied to will be glad to provide them
with small phials and instructions for collecting.

The kind co-operation of B.C. mountain climbers in
this matter would be greatly appreciated.[26]

Wailes knew that the cause of red snow in this cryoplankton community was a kind of algae, *Chlamydomonas nivalis*, and was most
prevalent in conditions above 5,000 feet. The iceworms "belong to the

order *Oligochaeta*, genus *Mesenchytraeus*."[27] These little beasts, appearing as "minute black slender forms from a quarter of an inch to one inch in length, with the thickness of a coarse black thread," were known to feed on the algae present in red snow.[28]

The trio then crossed the expanse of Dais Glacier to Regal Glacier, where they encountered the challenge of a *bergschrund*, a chasm between the glacier and the snow slope leading to the mass of the mountains. "We went straight up to the apex of a small peak about 11,000 feet high," Don Munday wrote. Afterwards, they "were now only level with the Dais Glacier, above which rises the immense south wall of the mountain, crowned at the nearer end with the impending blue cliffs of Epaulette Glacier. Forest fires dimmed distant views."[29]

They returned to base camp via Icefall Point and relayed more "grub."[30] By August 13 they were set, determined to travel east across Corridor Glacier. From a feature they named Glacier Island, Don Munday saw the ice stretched northeast farther along Corridor Glacier, and southeast along Agur Glacier, which flowed "from Mount Agur, named after A.E. Agur [*sic*], member of the 1926 expedition killed in an avalanche near Vancouver."[31]

Icefall Point camp in 1927 was a place of refuge in a sea of ice.

They climbed cliffs at Mount Jester to find an extraordinary little patch of grass at the 7,000-foot elevation, surprising all of them in this world of ice; the grass even presented some findings of sticks and served as a campsite. "By brilliant moonlight we left at 12:40 a.m., descending to the broken marginal ice of Corridor Glacier and working out to the middle where the longitudinal crevasses were completely masked by thin, brittle snow. The distance involved made it impracticable to sound with the axe at every step, so the leader was certain to break through frequently. Mrs. Munday assumed leadership on the return trip by moonlight."[32]

Not only was Phyl Munday taking the helm, she was also taking photographs. Throughout Munday's article "The Apex of the Coast Range" are several stunning photographs credited to Mrs. Munday. At a time when published photography was rarely, if ever, credited to a female climber, this was advancement of another sort.

The trio regularly encountered icefalls, which Don Munday described as "massive ruins" at one point, as though they were the remnants of an ancient, mighty civilization. Although perhaps beautiful to behold, these were serious impediments in their progress. Flimsy ice bridges furthered their progress. A distant forest fire sent smoke clouds into view. "Tawny smoke-clouds were now pouring over Spearman Peak and Mt. Munday from the north," Munday wrote. This is first mention of the over 11,000-foot peak named after the couple; the naming was the recommendation of G.G. Aitken, B.C. representative of the Geographic Board of Canada.[33] The name of the peak so near to Mystery Mountain was indicative of the rapid influence Phyl and Don Munday were having, not only on settler culture of the new province but also on a national identity firmly rooted in the conquering and classification of nature prevalent in the period. It was also a signpost to other mountaineers that glory, even a higher spiritual plane, could be found in this remote collection of glaciers and peaks.

As for this expedition with the Mundays and Betty McCallum, the sunlight, far from being a comfort, was proving to be a cause for trepidation, although the climbers met it with stoicism. They were continually exploring, trying routes that appeared to the eye as being most favourable, but battling "the heat of the day [that] was bringing down snow and rocks along the wall." Don Munday continued, "Both women were bruised repeatedly; Mrs. Munday's hair was matted with blood, and her arm severely bruised by interposing it toward a rock between her and her sister's head. Finally a place was reached where to have advanced would have violated the rudimentary principles of good climbing. And even had this danger spot been conquered it would have meant a night on a ledge at 11,000 feet before continuing the ascent."[34]

Rather than a defeat, their advancements in the region, as well as the knowledge gained when it came to terrain and climbing conditions, were a boon that would provide the Mundays with an understanding for future expeditions. The climbing party made several assessments that would increase the chances for the next team that passed into range of Mystery Mountain. "Fury Gap is not a true pass," Don Munday noted from a bivouac, as an example of determinations made in the 1927 foray, "the descent on the north to Scimitar Glacier being impractical."[35]

Occasionally emerging from the increasing forest fire smoke in a foreign, inhospitable land, the trio sought refuge in the heights.

> Going across the Gap to the base of the peak we named Mt. Chris Spencer [height 11,000 feet, named after a prominent member of the Alpine Club of Canada] we studied such unpromising parts as were visible of the great west ridge with its 10 peaks ranging in height from 10,000 to 11,500 feet. The north peak shone far away, 5,000 feet above us. From the immense basin enclosed by Mystery Mountain, Teidemann [*sic*] Peak and Mt. Hickson [named for Joseph William Andrew Hickson], Scimitar Glacier cascaded chaotically in two parallel icefalls for 2,000 feet into a curving valley that was savagely desolate in its utter lack of vegetation, the bare crags soaring from the glacier floor too sheerly, in most places, for snow to cling. These peaks between Mt. Spencer and Mt. Bell [named for then Alpine Club of Canada president F.C. Bell of Vancouver] promised excessively difficult rock climbs.[36]

These rapid namings would also feature Mount Geddes, named after the late Malcolm Daniel Geddes, the Alpine Club of Canada's honorary librarian of Calgary, who had died in a mountaineering accident near Mount Lefroy in 1927.[37]

Threatening avalanches. Deep crevasses. Daunting icefalls. Collapsing ice and rock. The overall impression from the 1927 expedition is that of an environment that was not only inhospitable but presented a climb of excessive danger and challenge, even to the experienced climber. Betty McCallum had to return to Vancouver, and after she left on the SS *Venture* on August 23, Don and Phyl Munday returned to their base camp to explore the region. But they encountered stormy weather and did not last long in their explorations.

One of the most overwhelming conclusions from this foray was that the newly named Franklin Glacier was the route in, and it would continue to entice the Mundays to return via the sea and up Knight Inlet. "Despite the necessity of 'man-packing' from sea-level, Mystery Glacier is the logical route. The region possesses considerable geological interest, but the time spent unravelling the intricate defenses of the big mountain prevented trips in other directions."[38]

The Mundays' efforts, along with Betty McCallum's, would not go unrewarded. This expedition and its results, published in the *Canadian Alpine Journal* and other publications of the period, would generate a kind of spiritual fervour that would border on the obsessive. It was not unlike the mania that had enveloped the Matterhorn in a mist of attempts and accomplishments, rendering its climb at times unstable and unsafe.

Phyllis Munday carrying a 70-lb. pack while traversing the Franklin Glacier in 1927.

CHAPTER 3:

BEYOND THE UNKNOWN

It was with great interest that the outside world followed the third attempt of Mr. and Mrs. Don Munday and Mr. Munday's brother, to scale British Columbia's loftiest peak, Mt. Waddington, 13,260 ft. Although beset with many obstacles and hardships this trio of climbers finally conquered Nature and reached the goal of their ambitions. They certainly deserve credit for the time and energy spent in the three trips into this country and the British Columbia Mountaineering Club is proud in the fact that two such climbers as Mr. and Mrs. Munday are members of our organization.[1]

—F.A. Spouse, "Mt. Waddington Conquered"

This was, of course, not true. The climbers had made it to the top of the northwest peak, from where they spotted the true summit.

In *The B.C. Mountaineer*, introduced now as a Fellow of the Royal Geographical Society, W.A.D. (Don) Munday presented "The Heart of the Coast Range."[2] From far away, Munday wrote, a climber will not spot that Mount Waddington, as it was now known, is made up "of some 20 peaks ranging from 10,500 to 13,260 feet."

> At the 10,000 foot level the massif for a length of six miles is nowhere below 10,500 feet, forming a wall-like mass between Franklin Glacier on the south, and Tiedemann and Scimitar glaciers on the north, the three flowing respectively southwest, eastward and northward, with a total area of fully 150 square miles; Franklin Glacier is over 20 miles in length, Tiedemann Glacier is 16 miles long, and Scimitar Glacier probably not less than 12 miles. Glaciers of equal size exist nowhere so far south of the Pole in the Northern Hemisphere except in the Himalayas.[3]

In the opening sentences of his description of the previous summer's expedition, Munday, with his new title, was already taking a global mountaineering approach, comparing the newly explored coastal range with the home of Everest, also yet to be ascended. He was also getting out to the membership of the BCMC the statistics he believed they were hungry for. Rumours had been circulating about the size of the mountainous country. In the second paragraph of his article in *The B.C. Mountaineer*, Munday wrote that there "are at least three peaks which are exceeded only by Mount Robson." He was pointing out that the scope of this area was larger than that in which the monarch of peaks within British Columbia was to be found. He also took pains to argue that the route established by him and his wife up the Franklin Glacier was the one true trail up to this new mountain of superlatives, and all rumours of other paths were to be quietened. "The route up the Franklin Valley, used in 1927 and 1928, is the logical entrance to the region, although there is a persistent myth that the Chilcotin country offers a better route. The distance from the mouth of the Franklin to Mystery Mountain in a straight line is only about 26 miles. The trip from Vancouver to the mouth of the Franklin took four days; the return took five."[4]

Phyl, Don, and his brother Bert were attempting this climb. The weather would prove to be uncertain, and this hampered their efforts. As Chic Scott writes, "It was not until July 7 that the three of them were once again bivouacked at Fury Gap."[5] Munday found the conditions for travel up-glacier much more satisfactory than the previous year. However, the meteorological conditions left much to be desired, despite their having a fair amount of time slotted in the calendar for the work. "In three weeks after establishing base camp we had only one whole day really fit for climbing the higher peaks," Munday lamented.[6] Nevertheless, the Mundays' confidence was high, even before they had left Vancouver. They were spring-loaded once that good-weather day arrived. "The weather had been extremely poor," Munday biographer Kathryn Bridge wrote, "with persistent rain and almost incessant wind. All three were frustrated and the enforced idleness challenged their patience. On the morning of July 8, just past 1:00 a.m., wind raged in Fury Gap, but they set out anyway, following their route of the previous year."[7]

The final tower of Mount Waddington, as seen from the northwest peak.

A panorama of the main tower of Mount Waddington and nearby peaks. The length of Franklin Glacier can be seen.

The climbers traversed Fireworks and Herald Peaks and passed Men-at-Arms, Bodyguard, and Councillor Peaks before arriving at the base of the final peak at 6:20 p.m. "In deep granular snow they plowed their way up, cutting steps in the ice beneath," Chic Scott wrote. "The summit came suddenly, a knife-edge crest which they were forced to straddle."[8] The conditions were reminiscent of the first ascent of Canada's tallest peak, Mount Logan, in 1925, led by A.H. MacCarthy and Fred Lambart. It was also similarly anticlimactic.

Don, Phyl, and Bert Munday, after exclaiming their excitement over their achievement, looked across to the southeast. There, across a chasm, was the true summit of Mount Waddington. Biographer Kathryn Bridge wrote,

> Phyl's comment summed it up. "It was such satisfaction [getting to the top] but we were absolutely aghast." They were not on the summit of Waddington as they

Franklin glacier   Mt Jubilee   W. Summit ↓

from Summit NW Peak   1928 + 34

had thought, but on an adjacent peak towards the northwest. The highest spire—mere metres from their reach—towered upwards another 60 metres. They were so close to the summit that they could differentiate the striation on it ... They were exhausted. After a brief 15 minutes "on that glorious crest," they turned down. It was a long all-night trek back to Fury Gap. They arrived about 2:00 a.m.[9]

Don Munday sought solace in the fact that at least from a geological standpoint, they had climbed the crux of the mountain, the top peak in the range. Although his explanation in the *Canadian Alpine Journal* read like an admittance of defeat, with some 20/20 hindsight thrown in Munday also framed it like the victory he'd expected. "The crest which we straddled has not been triangulated; though it is the culmination of the main mass of the mountain, there seems no doubt that the slender eastern pinnacle is a few feet higher. We had hoped to find it accessible from this side. No mountain yet attempted in Canada has such a well-guarded summit. As a consolation prize, our own summit was such a splendid conquest as to soften the disappointment of not reaching the very apex of the range."[10] They were simply too exhausted to attempt the challenging rock climb.

It would be a while before Don and Phyl Munday attempted Waddington again. "It would be another two years before they next returned," wrote Bridge. "The unexpected death of Phyl's mother in early 1929 may have put a damper on any inclination to climb."[11]

In 1930, the Mundays caught on to ski-mountaineering, for which Alpine Club of Canada member and new editor of the *Canadian Alpine Journal* Alexander Addison McCoubrey had advocated. Returning to the Coast Range, the Mundays this time came with equipment that would allow for easy and more efficient traverses of the vast snowfields and glaciers standing between the point of entry into the Coast Mountains and the achievement of the base of the summit peak.

It was apparent that the era of the ski-mountaineer was now at hand, with *The B.C. Mountaineer* going great guns about the new mountaineering sensation. "A knowledge of skiing, the king of all winter sports," began the February 1931 issue, "is now recognized by the world's most prominent climbers as a most essential factor to every mountaineer."[12]

Endurance was also a factor in mountaineering pursuits in remote areas. How much energy is expended simply in getting to the base of the mountain a climbing party wishes to overcome? How much food supply and equipment are exhausted? Does more time spent travelling mean risking the possibility of an adverse weather event that might prevent getting to a peak? Don and Phyl Munday must have been pondering these questions after their last foray to Waddington, and Don's modestly titled "Ski-Climbs in the Coast Range" certainly starts strongly in advocating for a pair of well-waxed skis as being a cheerful addition to anybody's kit when attempting the mysterious mountain. "Three seasons in the Mt. Waddington section of the Coast Range fully convinced us that ski [*sic*] were logical equipment to overcome the obstacles imposed by the immense snowfields. Faster travelling meant extending one's effective climbing range, thereby making it possible to take advantage of brief spells of favorable weather where unsettled weather naturally resulted from sea-winds sweeping up abruptly 10,000 feet across the glacial mantle of the range."[13]

Trapper Jim Stanton once again lent his assistance in transporting the Mundays by boat to the trailhead at the head of Knight Inlet. Two years previous, the Munday expedition that reached the northwest peak of Waddington had cached food at Icefall Point, which would serve as base camp. This patch of greenery in a maelstrom of ice and snow was now a traditional launching point. Once again, the weather was unpredictable, as Kathryn Bridge notes, "but on July 17 they ventured out late in the afternoon to try out their skis. They got to the top of Mount Redbreast (2,049 metres) behind camp, the lowest mountain in the district. It was nice warm-up for the remainder of the week. The following day, they ventured along the Franklin and Whitetip glaciers and skied and climbed Shelf Mountain. Next they carried their skis across the Franklin Glacier to Dauntless Glacier, until they found enough snow for continuous skiing."[14]

The traverse of large patches of ice and snow was required before getting to the climbing of a remote peak, and Don and Phyl Munday achieved one more notch in the buildup to an eventual successful climb up the final peak of Waddington: an equipment solution to the endurance question of getting to the mountain. After having spent days on their skis on their return down Franklin Glacier, Don asked his wife, from whom he regularly sought advice, what her official endorsement was for the use of skis in mountaineering. "'Were they worth it?' I demanded next day while my wife struggled to steer her ski through a trail-less thicket where the river had flooded the trail to the river mouth. 'Every bit of it!' she retorted without hesitation, even at such a moment."[15]

———•———

It was an unusual place for the Mundays to bump into Henry S. Hall Jr. The veteran climber of such expeditions as the 1925 first ascent of Mount Logan was strolling along the street in Vancouver when the three shook hands excitedly. What brought Hall to town? Well, funny they should mention that. Hall had planned an approach to Mount Waddington that would take his party up the Homathko River. Would Don and Phyl be interested in joining him on the attempt? Why, yes, they would. However, with banks closed over the weekend, finding the funding was a bit awkward for Don and Phyl. All was eventually worked out, and the Mundays found themselves steaming to Squamish at 9:00 a.m. on Monday, keen to join this ambitious American climber along with Alf Roovers, Don Brown, and Hall's Swiss guide Hans Fuhrer. This was how the 1933 Waddington trip began.[16]

In his thoroughly researched *Canadian Alpine Journal* article "High Peaks of the Coast Range," Don Munday wrote that although the area had been thoroughly explored, "my wife and I possessed a general knowledge of most of it and the chief gaps had been filled in by the 1932 expedition of Henry S. Hall, Jr., down the West Homathko river. So irresistible proved Mr. Hall's generous invitation to join him in 1933, that we prepared in less than a day and a half to leave Vancouver with him on June 26th."[17]

Thus began a new phase in climbing in the Mount Waddington area. Americans were now in. Alpine climbing had become a matter of international cooperation and a pilgrimage that crossed the forty-ninth parallel. This expedition would have the little group of mountaineers coming at Waddington from the northeast, which must have been a paradigm shift for the Mundays. Don Munday had sworn by the western approach, by sea, for years, and any "attack" on Waddington from the east was, in his view, not as effective as travel up Franklin Glacier.

"Our 1933 approach from Tatla Lake, down the west fork of the Homathko, up Scimitar Creek and Glacier, and ascent of Mt. Combatant for a view of the northeast face of Mt. Waddington had, with the Mundays' previous knowledge, gained for us certain valuable information," wrote Hall in the *American Alpine Journal*.[18] With this route firmly in mind, the group motored "22 kilometres along a rocky road to Bluff Lake where they met their wranglers: Pete Evjen, Pete McCormick and H.T. Valleu."[19]

It was on this expedition that Mount Waddington took on a new dimension for the Mundays. The mountain was now no longer just an objective; it had taken on elements of a deity, a spirit, or at the least, a companion.

Daylight lingered all night along the northern horizon. A waning moon drew an ethereal web over Waddington —to some of us more than a mere mountain, a presence perceivable. When sunrise flashed on that lofty crest at 4 a.m. we and all the mountain world crouched awhile longer in deep lilac shadows almost like coloured mist.

We now thought that from the main Scimitar ice-fall "Angel glacier" might be climbed without excessive risk to approach the "Munday summit" of Waddington and thence perhaps reach the main summit—in answer an ice avalanche with a front of 250 yards thundered, lost in dust clouds, across the chosen corridor. Frequently throughout the night avalanches had broken the awe-inspiring silence.[20]

Other factors would sway them away from an attempt on Waddington's main summit. Although rain was making conditions mushy, by

Members of Henry S. Hall's 1933 Waddington expedition, including Don and Phyllis Munday (middle, top row).

July 17 high winds were threatening to tear the tents apart. In his writing, Don Munday continued to personify the Waddington area, as though it was conspiring to keep them away from an assault on the final peak or sending spectres to dissuade them.

> I, at least, went to bed with fears for the tents. Phyl had sewn ours. It was merely a matter of time before the tents must chafe through where held down by rocks; the wind hardly impressed us as possessing extreme horizontal velocity; its blows seemed directed downward like an invisible beast trampling the tents. We concluded that strong local wind is normal on this section of the glacier.
>
> At 1 a.m. Phyl and I discovered an eighteen-inch slit in our tent. While we dressed and thrust things into our packs, two more opened. In hissing sleet we dropped the tent to avoid its complete destruction. We moved into the tent Hans [Fuhrer] occupied (cook tent by day). Though new, by 6 a.m. it split all one end and rain steadily soaked everything. The other tent had to be pierced to drain an inch or two of water off its floor. With Waddington unapproachable and Tiedemann almost in the same class, there seemed little merit in continuing to occupy the camp.[21]

With their spirits sodden along with their torn tents, they made their way down windy Scimitar Glacier, once again defeated.

In 1935, Henry Hall would sum up the experience in his article for the *American Alpine Journal*. "The principal approaches to Mt. Waddington have now all been worked out," he wrote with confidence. Incorporated into this assessment was a 1934 expedition that had yet to take place, and it began behind the wheel of a 1930 Plymouth. Hall wrote that "a Winnipeg party comprising Ferris and Roger Neave and Campbell Secord had come in from the east" and would at its conclusion make up "one of the finest attempts on any mountain in Canada in recent years."[22]

CHAPTER 4:
WINNIPEG

So it came about that after a year's scheming and a week's hard driving Campbell Secord, my brother Roger, Arthur Davidson and myself stood at the end of the last hundred and fifty miles of roughish road and looked down Tatlayoko lake into one of the deep portals of the range.[1]

—Ferris Neave, "New Ways to Waddington"

The Plymouth had been Ferris's pride and joy for four years. He had bought it new in 1930 for $920. It was now towing a small trailer, carrying a significant amount of gear for a journey west. It was still quite dark at 5:40 a.m. when they left the Secords' house. All the packing had been done the night before.[2]

"There'd been stories about Mount Waddington coming out from the Mundays for some time before we even considered climbing it," Roger Neave explained to Susan Leslie in a 1979 interview. "But it sounded like a fascinating mountain, and there'd been numerous attempts, in the order of ten or twelve attempts, to climb it before we seriously got the idea of having an expedition there."[3]

In many ways, the departure from the Secord home was an appropriate launching point for the quartet. Campbell Secord had gathered the knowledge they had of their destination. The equipment in the trailer, packed the night before, had also been listed and gathered by Campbell. "Campbell's patient and meticulous accumulation of data on the geography, meteorology and accessibility of the whole district, and the courtesy of the various officials and private individuals who attempted to satisfy his curiosity, were potent aids to our setting forth.

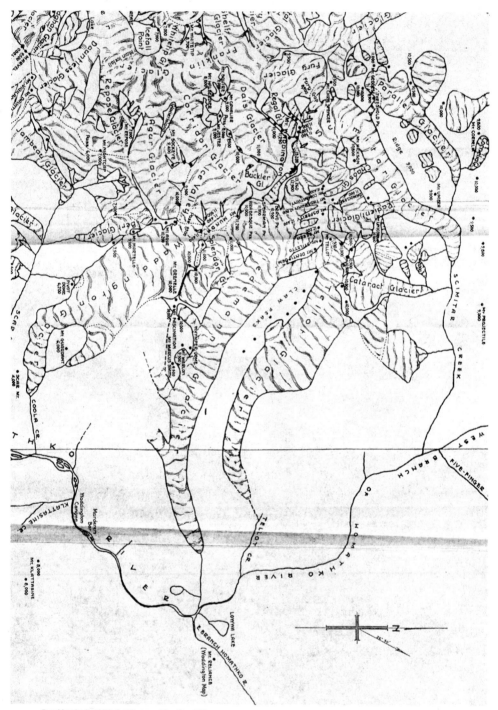

Don Munday's 1934 sketch map of the Coast Range.

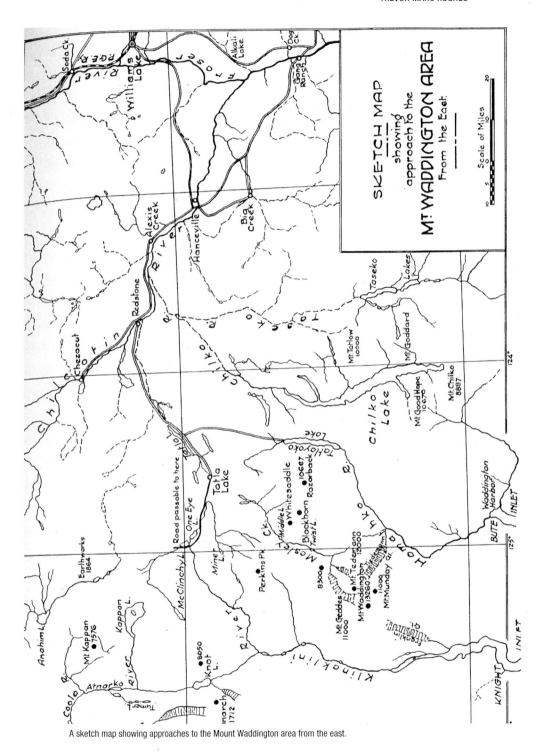

A sketch map showing approaches to the Mount Waddington area from the east.

To Campbell, too, fell most of the work of organising the material and equipment for our lengthy journey," wrote Ferris Neave in the *Canadian Alpine Journal*.[4]

Ferris Neave was documenting the journey. His diary writing was also meticulous. Married for less than two years to Marjorie Langdon Davis, thirty-three-year-old Ferris was a small, physically active, and intelligent young man with fair hair and complexion. With him was his younger brother Roger, twenty-eight years old, small yet strong of body, also of fair hair, and with an infectious enthusiasm for climbing. At only twenty-one years old, Campbell Secord was a young man you didn't want to argue with, with strong opinions, great endurance, and a sharp engineer's mind. Arthur Davidson was the least experienced climber of the group, but he was also enthusiastic. His boots were new, and so was his interest in mountaineering.

Roger sat in the front seat next to Ferris, with Cam and Arthur in the back seat. With a nod to all present, Ferris pushed in the starter pedal and turned the key in the ignition switch. The Plymouth rumbled and jiggled to life. Ferris pushed in the clutch pedal, then pushed the gearshift lever into first gear. The rumbling settled down, and they could feel the clutch plates come together. Ferris looked over his left shoulder and pulled out into the street.

"So what we planned to do (this all took place in Winnipeg), we planned to drive out from Winnipeg which we did carrying all our equipment and food supplies and so on for the whole trip on a small trailer," Roger later recalled. "We drove out from Winnipeg, this was during the Depression years. People thought we were farmers driving out from the dry belt."[5]

They bounced along in the dust, testing out the trailer hitch, en route to the highway. The day's plan was to drive west until they reached the boundary with Saskatchewan. The Plymouth was reliable as the heat of the day climbed increasingly higher, but it encountered strong resistance from a west wind. Soon after crossing into Saskatchewan, the first twisters were spotted in the distance, kicking up much dust and debris. Suddenly a loud bang rattled the foursome. It was too close to be related to the twisters, and they looked out the rolled-down windows to see they had their first puncture of the road trip.[6] This was not part of what they had planned for their Waddington expedition all through the winter months.

"All the previous attempts had been from the west, from the coast," Roger recalled years later, "up the inlets and some of the glaciers on the west side. It was a completely new idea to go in from the east. And this in itself was an attraction of course."[7] Roger was born in Cheshire and had come to Canada in 1928 when his brother Ferris, an entomologist, offered him a job in his freshwater fish assessment work at a biological station on a forty-three-foot schooner named *The Breeze* in Lake Winnipeg. Roger graduated from the University of Manitoba with a degree in electrical engineering and later found employment at Imperial Oil. Through a friend, A.A. McCoubrey, the Neave brothers became interested and experienced in mountaineering, although their early training grounds were in local rock quarries, which Roger found to be a "big help in rock technique." He remembered that his footwear while training consisted of "regular running shoes."[8]

The Winnipeg Section of the Alpine Club of Canada (ACC) was very active, and McCoubrey, its chairman, was a seemingly indefatigable individual. Winnipeg, of course, was where the ACC was founded by surveyor Arthur O. Wheeler and journalist Elizabeth Parker at a 1906 meeting.[9] Roger's first ascent had been in the Purcell Range of the Selkirk Mountains just west of Lake Windermere in British Columbia. During that first summer of climbing in 1929, he had ascended Mount Toby and Mount Redtop using only rope. "Rope could afford a lot of protection, even in those days, for everybody but the leader … pitons were not in common use," Roger recalled. "Mount Waddington was the first time I'd ever used a piton, I think."[10] Roger had climbed with his brother Ferris and Alex McCoubrey Jr., making a first ascent of Peak #4 in the Purcells in 1929. That same climbing season, without the use of rope, Roger showed his instinct for rock climbing by ascending Mount Louis alone. As Gil Parker put it in *Manitoba Climbers: A Century of Stories from the Birthplace of the Alpine Club of Canada*, "Even then Roger had shown his prowess as a rock climber. Behind Mt. Norquay above Banff is a limestone spire rising starkly out of the forest. Mount Louis, little-known to the public, provides a major challenge to mountaineers.

Overcoming the difficulties requires rock climbing skills and mind control; parts of the route hover above a 1,000 metre drop [almost 3,300 feet]. In that first season, Roger climbed Louis without benefit of rope or partners, a solo ascent!"[11]

The 1933 climbing season saw the Neave brothers particularly active. Roger made a first ascent of Molar Tower in the Rockies with Grahame Cairns and Alex McCoubrey Jr. two weeks before the Paradise Valley summer camp hosted by the Alpine Club of Canada. The Neave brothers combined their experience when, also in 1933, they went after a series of peaks in the Purcells. "That same year the Neave brothers reached the Leaning Tower group of mountains in B.C.'s Purcell Range," wrote Gil Parker. "They climbed several peaks along Kootenay Lake, and Roger first sighted the breath-taking granite spires east from Mt. Kaslo's summit. Their party forced their way up Campbell Creek, making first ascents of the spires along clean, but often narrow and steep granite ridges."[12] They had both moved on considerably far from the quarries outside Winnipeg, and they were hungry for more climbs. The winter of 1934 had them, fuelled by the recommendation of their mentor A.A. McCoubrey Sr., planning their adventure west.

———— • ————

They stopped for lunch in Carlyle, where they repaired their flat. Their readiness to smile and laugh covered their apprehension over what lay ahead. Ferris was keen to drive on, so without further delay they continued, curving into a northwest trajectory towards Moose Jaw. Twenty miles past the city, they stopped for the night and made their beds in a field. Ferris was impressed by their progress that day: 460 miles.[13] The Plymouth had done well.

May 28 started at 5:15 a.m.[14] The foursome struck camp rapidly. Gophers popped out of their holes, curious about the figures stowing away their stuff in the motorized contraption. The Plymouth began with a little choke applied because of the night's chill and cool morning air. Getting up to a little over ten miles an hour, the vehicle bounded down the road. The spirit of the men perked up with the rising of the sun behind them.

This was not the first road trip the Neave brothers had undertaken in the Plymouth with Campbell Secord in search of climbing adventure in British Columbia. In May 1932, a quartet of climbers arrived in Field, B.C., with their skis and poles. They discovered on the drive into Yoho National Park that the winter had generously distributed snow and "before reaching the switchbacks we were compelled to abandon the car and distribute the supplies among the four capacious pack-sacks. These were borne on the persons of A.A. McCoubrey [Sr.], my brother Roger, Campbell Secord, and myself," Ferris Neave later wrote.[15]

Under the guidance of "Mac," their nickname for McCoubrey, after getting to their camp at Takakkaw Falls they followed the Yoho Valley on their skis in the glorious winter sunlight until they had a spectacular view of the peaks of The President and The Vice-President. Leaving their skis behind, the three others followed Roger as he kicked steps to enable their ascent, and they found themselves on the summit of The Vice-President, just over 10,000 feet in height, at 5:45 p.m. on May 4. "The magnificent scenic effect of an evening sun on spring snows made us linger more than half an hour before starting down to our skis," wrote Ferris in retrospect.[16] These two days were a bonding experience, the Neaves building trust in a new partner, rock climber Secord, and furthering their connection with their mentor McCoubrey. They skied on through the darkness to their cabin.

Morse is a town named after the inventor of the telegraph. But on this day, the four adventurers were there to fuel up the car, get some milk, and find a sink where they could splash some water on their faces. They spotted more gophers as they pushed on. A magpie on the wing broke the monotony near Swift Current. The corrugated surface of the road shook the expedition vehicle from time to time. They even caught a glimpse of a coyote with a limp gopher hanging from its jaws as they neared Medicine Hat.[17]

Considering the miles they were covering, Ferris felt inclined to give his pride and joy some rest and relaxation. They found a garage and the Plymouth was set up with some lubrication, while the personnel of the expedition found some lubrication of their own at the Cecil Hotel.[18] The kitchen was open in the three-storey brick building, and the men consumed their beverages with the aim of beating the dust and the heat. The sight of the South Saskatchewan River was also a welcome sight; they noted the change in environment from arid to grassland to rolling hills. The day was still hot.

Passing the town of Bassano, the four fellows soon realized with a groan that they had another flat. This time the trailer tire was punctured. After pulling over, they all bent down to take a look and scratch their chins at the sight of the battered wheel. Campbell volunteered to hoof it back to the town for another tube as the one they were looking at was beyond salvage. When he returned, they resealed the trailer tire and pushed on in the still heat until they reached the outskirts of Calgary. Arthur Davidson's parents would give them all a place to sleep that night in the family home.[19]

The next morning, a later start had them setting out for Banff at 11:40 a.m. There they met Clifford White, a ski-mountaineer and photographer of renown. Ferris wanted to interview him, and they planned for a two-hour stopover while Ferris spoke with him. Cliff had been part of the Sir Norman Watson ski-mountaineering attempt on Mystery Mountain just a few weeks earlier, but he had not completed the ascent due to a knee injury. Before he joined that expedition party, he hadn't been to the Coast Range, but according to Watson's later account *Round Mystery Mountain*, "his knowledge of local conditions in the Rockies was certain to be invaluable and, as an expert photographer who had specialized in mountain scenery, he strengthened the Expedition greatly in that respect."[20] Neave knew that White was not a rock climber, but as part of a growing movement of ski-mountaineers, a tradition that began in the Alps with the Paulcke ski traverse of the Bernese Oberland in 1897 and was brought to prominence by influential authors such as Sir Arnold Lunn, White had gained notoriety, and he had Ferris's respect. His participation in the 1934 Waddington expedition with Watson, Beauman, and Camille was the most recent, but previous adventures had placed White firmly in the breast of the Canadian mountaineering community. As Sir Watson wrote, the journey White undertook in 1932 "with three companions, across the Columbia icefield from Jasper Park to Banff, a distance of some 220 miles, must rank as one of the great feats of pioneer ski-ing in the Rockies, comparable with Arnold Lunn's early work in the Bernese Oberland."[21] White had requested that Sir Watson join him in his "great feat" in 1932; however, travel complications prevented Watson from doing so. In 1934, Sir Watson was pleased to have White be part of his Waddington expedition personnel, but this time an injury prevented White from completing the expedition (what had begun as a mildly strained knee became a serious impairment). White passed along what information he could to Ferris. But the most impactful statement he made, having just returned from the land of the unconquered mountain, was that he didn't envy Neave and his companions.[22]

Meanwhile, *The B.C. Mountaineer* was going to the presses. The official organ of the B.C. Mountaineering Club was in its eleventh volume, the sixth publication of the year of 1934. Off the top were announcements about a summer camp confirmed "in the Black Tusk Meadows, Garibaldi Park, from August 4 to August 19," a report of a trip to Cathedral Mountain in the Rockies that "finished up as a glorious bush-whacking expedition," and an article about a rainy weekend trip in May to Mount Seymour. The members of this trip wished in the pages of the *Mountaineer* to "compliment those who have given their time to the erection of the Seymour Cabin, which has certainly added to the enjoyment of climbing on the mountain."[23] One page over, though, is a much shorter blurb: "An Attempt on Mt. Waddington." The snippet of two sentences briefly announced that "one of our best known climbers in the person of Alan Lambert is a member of a party of four who are leaving shortly for an attempt on that giant of the Coast Range, Mount Waddington or 'Mystery Mountain.'" Without delving into the complications inherent in what route was chosen or the strategic difficulties of the final tower— the nemesis of the Mundays—*Mountaineer* editor J.N. Betts chose brevity. "Alan may rest assured that the best wishes of the Club go with him and the party and that they return with a story of a successful ascent not only of Mount Waddington itself but of several other high peaks."[24] This was optimistic indeed.

Toba Inlet is a location of staggering beauty. Waterfalls gush off high cliffs, draining the glaciers of the surrounding mountains, turning the waterway pastel blue from the sediment added to the dark green seawater of Homfray Channel. As young climber Alec Dalgleish productively explored the peaks above the Toba River watershed during the summer months of 1933, the kernel of an idea began to grow in his head: an attempt on Mount Waddington the following season. The winter is the usual time to pore over maps and plan the exploits of the following season. Joining him in these plans was Alan Lambert, a prominent member of the British Columbia Mountaineering Club. Neal M. Carter and Eric Brooks, both members of the Alpine Club of Canada along with Dalgleish, had also been invited to join the expedition, which had high hopes of success. Carter, a regular climbing companion of Dalgleish who would later pen the account of the 1934 expedition (which was close to the same time as the Neave expedition), wrote "the writer was to journey south from Prince Rupert to Knight inlet in order to join the other three proceeding by chartered launch from Vancouver."[25] The quartet would meet at Glendale Cannery in a matter of days, following the same route undertaken by the Mundays. Neither the Dalgleish nor the Neave expedition team knew what the other was up to; in fact, neither knew of the other's existence.

The editor of the *Canadian Alpine Journal* at that time was A.A. McCoubrey (Mac), who was also serving as president of the Alpine Club of Canada. McCoubrey was based in Winnipeg, where Ferris Neave was serving as ACC's Winnipeg Section chairman. In his own account of the expedition, published in the pages of the *Canadian Alpine Journal* just before Carter's, Neave would open with compliments aimed at his Winnipeg colleague. "The initial stimulation to the adventure was supplied in great part by one A.A. McCoubrey," Neave wrote, "and was supplemented frequently by his sage and much-sought advice."[26]

Mac and Ferris got along well. Ferris saw him as a lone wolf although not by choice, and an enthusiastic hard worker. Mac did nothing by halves. "He was a thorough believer in the value of organization," Ferris wrote. "The threads of his interests run through the fabric of a score of clubs and societies," two of which included the Winnipeg Ski Club and the Dolomite Club of Winnipeg. "Soon after his arrival in Winnipeg Mac began to ski," Ferris wrote, "at a time when ski-ing was virtually unknown to Canadians except those of Scandanavian [*sic*] origin." The Dolomite Club of Winnipeg consisted of graduates, undergraduates, and staff at the University of Manitoba; members were also required to have proficiency in skiing and spend time climbing the walls of the quarries in Gunton, just north of Winnipeg. Mac was a determined climber who would often instigate solo expeditions during climbing seasons, and he had many ascents to his name. One in 1929 introduced a form of climbing that was new to many but had occupied Mac for some time already. "His climb of Mt. Vice-President in the spring of 1932 initiated ski-mountaineering in the Yoho region and he took part in its further development until 1941," Ferris wrote of his friend. "He was always at his best, indeed, in the company of younger people, whether they came to climb with him in the rock quarries in Gunton, to join in an evening's entertainment in town or, as men in the Services, to find a congenial haven in his hospitality."[27]

In 1929, in keeping with his appreciation of climbing companions of the younger persuasion, Mac had asked Ferris and Roger Neave to join him in a foray into the Purcells. The result was conveyed in McCoubrey's own contribution to the *Canadian Alpine Journal* of 1929, "A Purcell Pilgrimage."

> The alpinist of the future will, no doubt, be able to explain the fascination that the remoter parts of mountain ranges exert over mountaineers and why these mortals are willing to go back year after year and endure the discomforts of travel in trailless valleys, the doubtful pleasure of back packing and the weeping skies of the western ranges. To the present writer no convincing answer presents itself, but the fact remains that there is sufficient attraction to bring one back to more and more remote regions. To be sure, to balance the more

disagreeable physical aspects of travel, there is always the possibility of a companionship sufficiently attractive to make one forget the moments of misery.

It was the writer's good fortune, in planning another trip to the headwaters of the Hamill in 1929, to find in Ferris and Roger Neave, of Winnipeg, companions who possessed the necessary qualifications to offset the discomfort of any situation that might arise. Equipped with a fine technique in rock climbing, a comprehensive knowledge of Gilbert and Sullivan (sung occasionally off key, it is true), unfailing good humour and a kindly tolerance of the writer's efforts at humour, it seemed that nothing more could be desired. And so it proved.[28]

Thus was established a friendship in climbing and a mentorship that would further the Neave brothers' ambitions. Karl Ricker, a career geologist and an accomplished Canadian mountaineer who climbed with the Neave brothers in the 1950s, wrote this of the Neaves' mentor: "To no surprise of those who knew the irrepressible Alex [McCoubrey], a reconnaissance to investigate the potential of a ski mountaineering camp site area was launched in 1932. The frontline soldiers for the mission were the Neave brothers and a newcomer on the scene—a crack British rock climber, Cam Secord."[29]

As editor of the *Canadian Alpine Journal*, Mac had Ferris write for him; Ferris penned reviews in the early 1930s of ski-mountaineering titles such as Arnold Lunn's *The Complete Ski Runner*. In so doing, Mac brought Ferris into the fold of his intention to promote the new form of alpinism. But there was another bit of influence in which Mac was successful. "Alex McCoubrey convinced the Neave brothers that it was their turn to attempt Mt. Waddington, and by a route that the Munday entourage had so far not tested. The summer of 1934 was the targeted date for their attempt, early in the season, because there were at least two other parties scheduled to attempt it ..."[30]

As Ferris Neave drove, he contemplated what was ahead at Tatlayoko Lake. He and his expedition team were drawn not just by the road trip, which was an exploratory challenge in itself if only for the continual tire punctures, but by the idea of attempting something that had never been tried before. The routes explored by the Mundays, the documented inroads from Knight Inlet, were known. But from the east, the Homathko Valley to Tiedemann Glacier presented a tantalizing opportunity, at least from what Ferris and Roger could discern from their reconnaissance from the earlier expeditions. If anything, the east route looked simpler. Rowing the length of Tatlayoko Lake, travelling along the Homathko River, and the straight shot of Tiedemann seemed a kind of tonic for the nautical haul into Knight Inlet, the tramp up Franklin Glacier, and the windswept turn at Fury Gap before the attack on the peaks from the northwest, never mind the challenge at the final tower. What awaited them? Ferris stared out the dusty windshield with a searching gaze, the Plymouth bouncing along, the others quiet and contemplative as well.

The Plymouth and trailer were now dwarfed by the Rockies. The dramatic angular bulk of Mount Rundle impressed them all. Banff National Park had been renamed in the same year of production as the Plymouth from its previous designation as Rocky Mountains Park. The Banff–Windermere Road beckoned as they progressed along the glacial-silt blue of the winding Bow River, a regular travel companion that would wander off for a time before returning to guide their way. They turned left and soon crossed into British Columbia, where they became surrounded by high-sided coniferous forest, drawing the eye farther up the surrounding peaks. Mount Whymper's strata were pleasing to behold, and the car bounded to the southeast for the first time. The skies darkened in the south, where lay their goal for the end of the day, Radium Hot Springs. Dramatic cliffs appeared as they descended into darkness. About eight miles beyond Radium, which was reached at 8:30 p.m., the four decided to camp. The rain began to pelt the Plymouth, becoming heavier before they found a camping spot. While the men were setting up camp, the Plymouth's fuse blew, plunging them into complete darkness.[31]

Soon after rising at 7:30 a.m. and eating a basic breakfast, the group agreed to fuel up the car and themselves in Cranbrook. "We had to go over the Crowsnest Pass as the Banff route wasn't open at that time,"

Roger Neave later recalled.[32] The Banff–Windermere Road had sufficiently punished the tired tires of the trailer, the gear weighing it down
giving no reprieve, and a trailer tire blew before Yahk, where they mended
it. Then, before they could sufficiently recover from that mishap, yet
another trailer tire blew. Now the men were even more frustrated, and
after unloading the contents of the trailer in haste, they got down on
their hands and knees to fix it on the spot. They had a ferry to catch
across Kootenay Lake soon after Gray Creek.[33]

The previous night's rain had wreaked havoc just south of the lake.
Flooding was visible across the road and in surrounding towns, a deep
contrast to the dusty traverse of the plains just a few days before. The
cost for the passage for the car, trailer, and Ferris was three dollars, with
an extra twenty-five cents for Roger, Cam, and Arthur. The Plymouth
was loaded onto the modest watercraft for the crossing of Kootenay
Lake, and at 2:30 p.m. the vessel began puttering across to Balfour,
arriving about an hour later. From Balfour they dealt with alternating
rain and sun until they reached their next crossing point of the Kootenay River, where an on-call ferry with no charge took them across. Tire
issues continued to dog them: once they arrived in Nelson, the Neave
brothers realized with a groan that they had left their spare tires on the
ferry to Balfour. Roger and Ferris got back into the Plymouth, drove
back to Balfour, and waited for the return of the ferry before they apol-
ogetically claimed their lost automotive property. At Balfour, the Neaves
learned of a quicker, alternative route to get to Kamloops that would
take them through the town of Nakusp, travelling west through the
community of Vernon. With this news they returned to catch up with
Cam and Arthur in Nelson.[34]

Now firmly established in the Selkirk Mountains, the group decided
to call it a day a few miles north of the southern shore of sweeping Slocan Lake.

———•———

The attempt of a new route up Waddington was precipitated and
encouraged by the potential of the glacial routes from the east. As Ferris
Neave wrote later in the *Canadian Alpine Journal*: "Of the three tremen-

dous glaciers which radiate from the mountain, two, the Franklin and Scimitar, had so far not permitted parties to gain a footing on the higher, southeast peak. Tiedemann glacier might provide access to the east ridge or north face of this part of the mountain."[35]

The Neave brothers, Campbell Secord, and Arthur Davidson were following in some impressive footsteps. Not only had Don and Phyllis Munday devoted successive climbing seasons to exploring the Coast Range, but the road trip expeditioners also had another major mountaineering figure to thank for pointing out the route they were about to explore: Mount Logan expedition alumnus Henry S. Hall Jr. In the decade between the quest for Logan and the current quest for Waddington, Hall had made quite an impact in the world of mountaineering, and in the previous years had published his work in both the *American Alpine Journal* and the *Canadian Alpine Journal*. He became a member of the American Alpine Club in 1918 and never looked back. In the 1933 edition of the *Canadian Alpine Journal*, he penned "The Coast Range from the North and East," after the initial September 1931 adventure, bringing him to the Waddington Range from a new direction. He considered himself "privileged to do so" when "despite almost continuous bad weather, a glimpse of the Waddington group was gained from a hill on the north side of Mosley creek (known locally always as the Homathko, either west or north fork), at a point five miles northwest of Middle lake." The Plymouth was pointed in the direction of the Homathko Valley.

The *Canadian Alpine Journal*, volume XXI, contained an obituary written by Hall for Allen Carpe, who had perished on Mount McKinley that season, but who had also climbed with Hall on Logan in 1925. A.A. McCoubrey also contributed an article. McCoubrey was president of the ACC and editor of the *Canadian Alpine Journal* for volume XXI in 1933. He had been chairman of the Winnipeg Section from 1925 to 1932 and made the transition to president of the Alpine Club of Canada in 1932. Within that span, from 1928 to 1930, he had been vice-president of the Alpine Club of Canada as well as part of the Hut committee, restoring the Elizabeth Parker Hut at Lake O'Hara.[36] He was a busy man, devoted to the ACC, and was somewhat of a mentor to the Neave brothers. "After arriving in Canada from the United Kingdom in 1928, Roger and his brother Ferris lived in Winnipeg where they came under the tutelage of Alex McCoubrey, Sr. As editor of the *Canadian Alpine Journal*, and later president of the Alpine Club of Canada, McCoubrey was himself a very active climber. Roger made his first trip to the Rockies in 1929, with very limited experience gained in rock quarries near Winnipeg."[37]

————◆————

May 31 began early for the expedition. The Neave brothers, Cam Secord, and Arthur Davidson were up at 4:00 a.m. and on the road by 4:40. Ferris marvelled at the scenery as he drove along Slocan Lake. He was remembering the 1929 expedition with McCoubrey and Roger, which had also begun with a road trip along the Windermere Road. The scenery had been extraordinary too, and the approach by car a gradual introduction to the landscape. The Slocan was a sublime place. Although heavy rains had made the road hazardous and slippery in places, the four were in awe of the spectacular views above the lake. The quartet dined in Vernon, keen though to push on to Kamloops. But they managed to get only thirty-two miles west, where they hastily set up camp.[38]

On June 1, the four men wasted no time in driving into Kamloops. There they picked up their mail, found a bakery for a loaf of bread, and resumed their progress on the road north to Williams Lake. Light rain and cooler conditions prevailed until the sky cleared in the afternoon. The Plymouth reached a high point, and to the men's right Mount Robson came into view far away.[39] This was the former champion of British Columbia peaks, summited in 1913, which Mount Waddington had now superseded. The race was on to conquer the new peak.

They were now just a few miles from 100 Mile House.

CHAPTER 5:

TATLAYOKO LAKE

Beauty is as necessary to a man as food and drink. Spiritually, he cannot exist without it. He must have it in some form, whether it is music, art, literature, philosophy or religion. The hills are beautiful. They are beautiful in line and form and colour; they are beautiful in their purity, in their simplicity and in their freedom; they bring repose, contentment and good health.[1]

—F.S. Smythe, *The Spirit of the Hills*

"I am the very model of a modern major general," Ferris Neave suddenly began to sing. As if spurred on by an external force, Roger Neave leaped in with "I've information vegetable, animal, and mineral." Then, with a laugh apiece, Campbell Secord and Arthur Davidson attempted to chime in, their rote knowledge of Gilbert and Sullivan's rapid lyrics not as polished as the Neave brothers'. The laughs continued as they stumbled over the words, eventually trumping all of them, building the camaraderie of a risky enterprise. It was moments like this that lightened the contemplative mood as they looking out at the passing landscape, often ruminating on what was ahead of them.

A stop at Williams Lake had them fuelling up the Plymouth and picking up a few provisions. Although it was evening, they decided to push on, proceeding south, then west. Tucking into their provisions, they had a rudimentary supper before taking on the darkness. They drove into the valley of the Fraser River, which included a steep climb for the Plymouth including a few switchbacks. Setting up camp about thirty-five miles west of Williams Lake, the young men looked forward to turning in, but in the back of their minds was the local knowledge, picked up in Williams Lake, that because of mud the road ahead was impassable. Maybe with a good night's sleep and more light, the way forward would present itself.[2]

June 2 saw them on the road by 6:30 a.m. They could now catch glimpses of the Coast Range, which generating excitement among them. They commented on how high and snow-covered the peaks were. In contrast to the pristine appearance of the nearing mountains, the road was a quagmire thanks to the recent heavy rains. "Oh, I am a pirate king!" Ferris began singing. In a deep, exaggerated baritone, Roger Neave continued, "... and it is, it is a glorious thing to be a pirate king!" Soon the crew were giggling like schoolboys.

The adventure beckoned, but their progress was extremely slow, largely due to the tire punctures. One of the overloaded trailer's tires, because of a casing that had seen better days, experienced four blowouts. The Plymouth was now covered in streaks of mud and was struggling to get the men across the trying landscape. Deep mud had them pushing the car and the trailer separately after detaching the trailer to make any progress.[3] It was exhausting. Repairing a tire in mud was not a pleasant experience, but perhaps there was a silver lining. Admiring the extraordinary view while having a break from mending tubes compensated for some of the inconvenience and frustrations of travelling by road. The peaks they viewed appeared dauntingly high. "And the road in, if you could call it a road, ends at Tatlayoko Lake. We were the first car to get through that last part of the way because of a few days of rain. And in many places we had to unhitch the trailer and manhandle the car through the mud holes and then manhandle the trailer through the mud holes and get going again."[4]

Once they reached the junction of Tatlayoko Road at Tatla Lake, they pointed the Plymouth's headlights due south. It was beginning to darken, and the mud continued. After some bumpy and hair-raising driving, Ferris, behind the wheel, began to spot structures, one of them the post office at the small community of Tatlayoko Lake. They were now deep in Chilcotin country, and it was nearing 10:00 p.m. As they proceeded towards the lake itself, their vehicle once more became bogged down in the mud, and pushing did no good. The men were exhausted from their travels that day and were ready to quit for the night. They slept right there, vowing silently that in the morning they'd find their way to Tatlayoko Lake, their gateway to the Waddington Range. At one point Roger had to run into the bushes, retching, sick to his stomach. The creature comforts were somewhat lacking.

Their plan for the following day was to cross Tatlayoko Lake. If successful, the four would follow the Homathko River, which was easier said than done. Survey parties had been to the upper part of the river in 1875 and 1928, but only a rudimentary understanding existed to guide the four climbers in.[5] If all went well, the long tongue of ice of the Tiedemann Glacier would provide them with a clear route into the lair of the Waddington Range. The foursome were inspired to continue because "the mere fact that no man had yet attempted this tremendous approach was in itself a sufficient challenge to the exploratory instincts of the party."[6]

But first a rescue operation had to be attempted. After a fitful sleep, the men stretched and yawned, Roger having borne the brunt of a poor rest, before trying to extract the Plymouth from the mud. The hole the Plymouth had entered proved to be a stern adversary, but much pushing from Cam, Roger, and Arthur, with Ferris at the wheel, saw them eventually free the car from the recess.

"Spent an hour prying the car out of the hole," wrote Ferris in his diary. "Then (8:00 a.m.) drove on to Ken Moore's," where they had planned to meet Jim Shields. Moore was the "pioneer rancher of Tatlayoko Lake."[7] Jim Shields was to assist the expedition party in transporting their gear to the south side of the lake with the aid of pack horses.[8] But the four climbers had to travel the remaining distance to Moore's house on their own. They unloaded the trailer of its heavy burden and detached it from the Plymouth at the lakeshore. Jim Shields was nowhere to be found, neither at Ken Moore's place nor anywhere nearby.

After a brief discussion, Cam and Ferris drove another six miles looking out for Jim Shields. Without him, the climbing party would not have much success after their crossing of the lake; they needed his packing expertise. At length they encountered him down the road and got out to greet him. Friendly and unassuming, Jim assured them he could start "almost immediately."[9] The men were relieved, and after much shaking of hands with their new packer, they attempted to start the Plymouth, to no avail. "Trouble with car," Ferris wrote in his diary, "+ after spending several hours on her, abandoned her + walked back to Tatlayoko Lake after a large meal at Bethany's (where Jim Shields lives). Family there like all other people here, very cordial and pleasant."[10]

After a brisk stroll back to Roger and Arthur, they found Roger much improved from his stomach troubles. He had assisted Arthur in the loading of a skiff they had rented and would row down the lake to where Jim Shields agreed to meet them with the pack horses. They had secured the rowboat in a little lagoon away from the wind, which was picking up. Roger later recalled, "Rowed the length of Tatlayoko Lake, which is about 14 miles."[11]

Ferris quickly learned from Jim that Tatlayoko Lake was often windy. An earlier breeze had picked up and now met them as a strong gale. Whitecaps appeared with startling frequency. Could this be a lake? It was like a small sea with the imposing mountains of the Coast Range just beyond, about a mile across in width west to east, and fourteen miles in length. It was a daunting landscape. Many of the trees near the lake had their tops permanently bent away from the lakeshore. First they would have to make it down the lake, and they wasted little time thinking about it. They had planned to row in shifts of two and take it as it came. The skiff was fully loaded, and they hoped it was ready and able.[12]

They pushed off from shore at 7:30 p.m. The swells gathered strength. With the wind against them, the fourteen miles down the lake to the mouth of the Homathko River seemed an inconceivable distance to row. The wind would abate but then pick up again, the skies not promising any relief. Ferris thought it to be quite an unsettled environment. After four and a half hours of constant rowing, they were twelve miles south of their starting point, and the party decided on camping at a point on the western shore.[13] After dragging the skiff up onto a beach, the men prepared themselves for a makeshift camp set up away from the wind, started a fire, and placed their bedrolls.

They enjoyed a modest sleep-in, emerging from their slumber just before 9:00 a.m. After a quick breakfast, they efficiently rolled up their camp and pushed the skiff out into the water. The lake was calmer than the previous day and the sunshine promised warmer weather. They kept up their shiftwork, in increasing awe of the towering peaks visible ahead, many of which they knew "reach an altitude of over 10,000 feet and are very beautiful in form. The whole scenery is at least equal to some of the highly advertised lakes of the Canadian Rockies."[14]

Their destination was the home of a man known locally as "Feeny" at the south end of Tatlayoko Lake. He was building a substantial log house, which would act as a warehouse of sorts for provisions to aid in his ambition to initiate a mining operation. The four men reached this site by 11:00 a.m. and found Feeney to be a quite congenial sort of fellow, with a kind demeanour and calm face. It was here that they would wait for Jim and the pack horses. Brown stoneflies had come out from the lake in full force that morning, Ferris noted as he swatted a few away. He knew Jim would take the pack horses down the east side of the lake, but he was not sure what his time of arrival might be. Luckily, they could bide their time with the friendly Feeney, and some of them even indulged in a swim in the lake, followed by a good meal.[15]

At about 3:15 p.m. Jim emerged with four pack horses. The climbing party was eager to begin after their refreshing afternoon, but they heard from their packer that it would be best to start out fresh the next morning, as the horses had travelled hard that day. After a brief conference, the men decided to camp and did some reconnaissance by the small tributary they called Feeney Creek (officially called the Ottarasko), which they would have to cross next day with the horses.

As Roger Neave later recalled in his interview with Susan Leslie, "We had arranged for a few pack horses to meet us at the other end and take us as far as they could down the Homathko valley. ... The Homathko valley cuts right through the Coast Range out to the Pacific. We were planning to go down the Homathko valley and then up Tiedemann Creek and Tiedemann Glacier. Tiedemann Glacier flows down from the east or southeast side of Mount Waddington."[16]

Keen to set out, the crew rose at 4:15 a.m., rounded up the horses, and enjoyed breakfast before loading the gear from the skiff onto the horses' backs and setting out on foot at 7:10. The initial travel was relatively simple: heading down into the valley, getting used to the accompaniment of beasts of burden. In total there were four pack horses, the riding horse on which Jim was mounted, and a colt. The scenery was extraordinary. The terrain was open and easily traversed.[17]

However, they soon encountered opposition in the form of harsh winds, and the entire party suddenly had to depart from easy meandering to courageous bouts of bravado. The recent rains appeared to have also contributed to the weakening of root systems, causing the collapse of many an old-growth tree. To further complicate their passage, the party and horses had to negotiate their way through thickening bush. It seemed that each time a particular path was chosen, a new obstacle presented itself. Ferris was impressed with the abilities of the pack horses. Overcoming nearly impassable terrain, the creatures seemed aware of the challenges of this particular section of travel.[18] This struggle tested the mettle of the climbers, limbering them up for what was to come— more of the unknown.

Roger Neave described it this way in an interview: "Nobody had been up this glacier before, and very few people had even been up or down the Homathko Valley before. There had been one railway survey party back in the last century when they were surveying for the CP Railway, and there had been a B.C. Hydrographic Survey come through there in the middle '20s. As far as we could find out, these were the only parties that had been through the Homathko Valley before."[19]

At slightly more than 2,300 feet, the party reached a survey camping ground and stopped to set up their beds for the night. It was 5:00 p.m., and camp was set up in contemplation. The entire party knew that the horses, despite their formidable abilities up to this point, would not be able to weather the terrain much farther: the Homathko was flooding its banks from the incessant rains. A logjam was visible ahead. The trail might not even be passable for human travellers soon. Their thoughts descended on alternative routes, and they couldn't help but wonder whether this route from the east was going to be a failed venture. Upon more thought, they decided the chances of the horses being able to go even a few hundred yards farther were very slim indeed, and they stopped for the night.[20] The pack horses were left to their own devices that evening while the men settled pensively into their bedrolls.

With June 6 starting well because of Jim Shields's efforts rounding up the horses and starting the campfire to prepare breakfast, the outlook of the four climbers improved. However, even after a good night's rest, their concerns about the terrain ahead had not abated. The decision was sombrely reached that Jim would have to turn back with the horses, the terrain being far too difficult for their passage ahead. With breakfast eaten, Jim prepared to turn back, and the horses' loads were removed and deposited on the ground. All shook hands with the packer before he led the beasts back the way they had come.[21]

Ferris, Roger, Cam, and Arthur now sorted through piles of equipment and had to make some decisions: what to take and what to cache. Before them lay "500 or 600 pounds of baggage that had to be transported down the Homathko Valley."[22] They cached a great deal of it high up in the cedars. They struck camp and with backpacks loaded, they commenced their traverse downriver, almost immediately negotiating steep banks and landslides as they made their way west.[23]

Despite their pioneering work on their current trail, Ferris Neave knew they had had some help in establishing it:

> Very few men have followed the course of the Homathko from Tatloyoko [*sic*] lake to the forks since the Canadian Pacific surveyor Marcus Smith and his six Indian packers went through in 1875. A Provincial hydrographic survey party covered the route in 1928 and since then August Schnarr, late of Bute inlet, has trapped marten successfully in this part of the valley during the winter months. The blazes and improvements which these travellers had left were a great help to our party in what is at best a very strenuous, though exceedingly interesting journey.[24]

The climbing party knew of August Schnarr, "a German American of high repute."[25] His status was highlighted in the writing of Don Munday, who had not seemed to know the full extent of his reputation before he and Phyllis did their reconnaissance of the Homathko River Valley in 1926. "In later years we came to realize August Schnarr was a half-legendary figure along the coast and in fact throughout the Coast Range for his strength, hardihood and skill as hunter, trapper and woodsman," Munday wrote in *The Unknown Mountain*.[26] The Neaves were continuing something of a tradition, with the Mundays having followed August Schnarr's advice in their 1926 exploration of the area.

One of August Schnarr's trapping cabins near the head of Bute Inlet, Homathko River Canyon, in the 1920s.

As Judith Williams points out: "August's expert handling of backcountry hazards contributed to the wilderness reputation that led pioneering coastal mountaineers Don and Phyllis Munday to seek his advice."[27] Schnarr's knowledge and resulting infrastructure had also helped out in other ways, with Mundays having "used August's local knowledge and trapping cabins he had built up the Homathko Valley for the first assault on the 4,019-metre (13,186-foot) Mt. Waddington, the highest mountain completely within British Columbia."[28]

The four men continued their trudge west on June 6. Their packs were close to eighty pounds each, and with landslides and steep cliffs at every turn, not to mention the high-water level in the Homathko, they were pushed off the easier route and "on to higher and rougher ground. … This was some of the roughest country I'd ever been in where back packing is concerned," Roger reflected in 1979.[29]

The mosquitos became more aggressive. Unaccustomed as they were to fresh blood, they swarmed the men at times, who were surprised by their size. The party stopped at 6:00 p.m., finding another survey party camp where they pitched tents and made their beds for the night. The mosquitos reduced their attacks in the following hour.[30] The next morning after breakfast, the foursome returned to the previous day's camp and picked up their first cache. There they had lunch and returned back to their tents with their loads.

It was at about this time that Ferris began to further his observations of local fauna. With mosquitos becoming an increasing nuisance, and in the interests of informing future expeditions into the Homathko, he created a simple chart in the back of his diary. Indicating the date, the time the beasts stopped biting, the temperature in Celsius, and the weather conditions, the measurements were an attempt, through empirical data, to note when the horrible creatures stopped eating mountaineers alive. On June 5, Ferris wrote that the biting ended at 9:00 p.m., with the mercury dipping to 11°C and clear weather. June 6 featured a slight variation, with the biting ending a half hour later, but the thermometer reading 13.2°C. Would a pattern emerge? Might there be a subject of study, fit for inclusion in the pages of the *Canadian Alpine Journal*? More in line with the gathering of traditional data, on June 7 Ferris took further notes on his observations of the local fauna. "2 goats + a kid," he scribbled, "3 lizards, 1 porcupine, several ruffled grouse with young chicks."[31]

Noting that the river was a little higher than the day before, Ferris and his companions set out with Roger in the lead, with the loads of their relay from the day before, just before 10:00 a.m. At first they encountered forest and bush, with devil's club appearing in growing quantities. Ferris observed that it "is less continuously obstructive than certain valleys in the Selkirks." After a stop for lunch, they entered Shelter Canyon. The environment was forbidding. "The bush wasn't too bad. Rockslides were terrible. They were one of the big difficulties, rockslides. And there were lots of canyons on the river too. ... [We] had to climb out of the valley to get round these canyons. ... Another of the problems was in some of the creeks. At that time of the year there was a lot of snowmelt from the mountains ... the creeks were all in flood. They presented a problem in one or two cases."[32]

Progress would now be impeded by "the height and frequency of the cliffs along its [the Homathko River's] banks and the general roughness and steepness of the terrain."[33] This is where the infrastructure of two survey parties and potentially, the trapping adventures of August Schnarr, played a part in their overcoming the hostile landscape. "Rickety ladders and logs" gave them a leg up in places, but in general the high-water level had them wading in deep, pushing them off the course of their predecessors and "on to higher and rougher ground."[34] They added one more bridge, having to fell a tree ahead of achieving their cache location. The men turned back at 5:35 after "a spot to eat."[35] There were more loads to transport to the cache, located at a rock slide. Ferris continued to note the evening activity of the mosquitos. He scribbled in his diary that they were "bad in places during the day" but "moderated about 7 or 8 P.M. + had almost stopped biting when we turned in."[36]

More relaying of their cache was ahead on June 9, with a 12:15 start after a sleep-in, getting "3 food units + 2 cans of gasoline, making 4 light loads."[37] Roger and Ferris carried their skis, with Ferris noting their return back to camp of origin in less than two and a half hours. The mosquitos had become worse, and the river rose even higher than before.

As their original camp had to be struck, the crew got up at 7:15 a.m. on June 10. They departed at 10:00 a.m. with what they could carry on their backs, going beyond their cache and camp, and learning that what lay ahead was "rocks + bush."[38] Optimism was restored when they discovered a trail, a ladder, and a fixed rope indicating previous human passage. But clearly previous winter floods had done their work, with trunks of alder and birch wrenched out by the roots and thrown into a massive pile, blocking their path. There was nothing for it but to break out the axes and start hacking their way through. Roger and Ferris decided to push on via a detour while Cam and Arthur continued their trek without the encumbrance of their packs to Nude Creek. "This is the largest tributary which the river receives on the northwest side between Tatlayoko lake and the forks," wrote Ferris Neave in the *Canadian Alpine Journal*, "and a glance at its seventy-five-foot width of white water showed that it would call for heroic efforts to get ourselves and our loads to the other side."[39] The river's thundering torrent, so strong that it physically picked up boulders and tossed them along, indicated that it was not time to ease up. The Neave brothers returned to meet Arthur and Cam, who had hacked a path through the windfall, and the four camped at Nude Creek at 7:40 p.m. With the path ahead made difficult not only by the rough water but also by more vertical walls of canyon, a method would have to be construed to ensure farther passage west.

On June 11, pushed out of their tents late in the morning by the heat of the sun, they got to work mending their pack boards and began to build a bridge across the creek.[40] June 12 dawned clear and pleasant, with American dippers (*Cinclus mexicanus*) flitting nimbly along the river as well as "4 dark ducks, with white eye spot very much at home in the rough water," Ferris noted in his diary.[41] These ducks, possibly harlequin ducks (*Histrionicus histrionicus*), would take to the air before dramatically plunging under the water's surface. But the men could not take to wing as the ducks could, nor did they fancy a plunge into the frigid waters, so the climbing party continued bridging Nude Creek. Two days would be devoted to this task.

"The main piece was a long, slender spruce tree," wrote Ferris in the *Canadian Alpine Journal*, "braced and supported by an intricate arrangement of poles and ropes. Its appearance did not flatter the two engineers in our party, but at least it worked."[42] A thin steel cable that Roger had tracked down in the forest, presumably left behind by one of the survey parties, served as a conveyor of materials, allowing the packs to be slid along for safe passage to the other side of the creek.

It was now June 13. Relaying their caches continued to be a necessary part of this buildup stage to the approach to Tiedemann Glacier. Cam and Ferris returned to their second camp, the one before Nude Creek, retrieving more equipment and sustenance. By 8:45 a.m. they had left that camp for the return journey.

With lunch and a halt of momentum came the fierce gathering of mosquitos. The repast was a rapid affair, and within the hour they were back on their feet. Ferris noted in his diary the sighting of several lizards and a Steller's jay, "indigo with pronounced crest."[43] Cam and Ferris reached Nude Creek at 6:45 p.m. They had arrived back at the camp before Roger and Arthur, who had taken more loads ahead and done some reconnaissance by exploring the trail ahead on the other side of Nude Creek. Roger and Arthur arrived back at Nude Creek camp at 7:15 p.m. Ferris wrote in his diary of a "difficult piece of cliff" ahead, one for which "packs had to be hoisted owing to high water making trail impassable."[44]

The next morning, June 14, they struck camp and focused on the work of packing and moving equipment and supplies along the wire cable—"the relic of the survey party"—over Nude Creek. After caching some of those items and eating lunch, the party then took up the rough trail, encountering several rock slides that had to be scrambled across.

The next body of water to be crossed was Bellamy Creek. This tributary of the Homathko was some distance down the valley. What they found when they reached it was a sight for sore eyes: it had already been bridged by an earlier snow slide, which the party used to cross over. The slide, which appeared to have happened recently, had "played havoc with the trees on both sides of the stream," leaving a scrambled, splintery mess.[45]

Although no formal pecking order had been established among the mountaineers, Roger was considered the leader, and his reconnaissance allowed for a more expedient traverse and hauling of packs. The water had risen to an impassable level farther downstream, but the "sensational cliff route" he had explored the day before was of great help to them. Once they were at the cliff, the party could see the withering, weathered poles that the 1875 Canadian Pacific Marcus Smith survey party had most likely used as ladders to achieve the upper parts of the cliff, with the guidance and help of Smith's six First Nations guides. The Neave expedition took the hint and, according to Ferris's written account in the *Canadian Alpine Journal*, the climb was achieved "by chopping down a tree and using it as a ladder against the rock face."[46] In both his published article in the *CAJ* and his diary, Ferris Neave pays homage to human ingenuity of both European and Indigenous origin, whether as a result of the Marcus Smith survey of 1875, the province's 1928 hydrographic survey, or the ongoing trapping efforts of August Schnarr. "Throughout this part of the journey we could not but be impressed by the masterly economy of material with which our predecessors had overcome the difficulties of the way. Here a couple of horizontal poles would carry us round a projected corner of cliff, there a notched tree trunk would elevate us to a new line of progress."[47] As Ferris noted in his diary, "couple of poles = trail or bridge, one pole with notches = ladder."

Finding a campsite now became a problem as they made their way far above Bellamy Creek. The climb was steep, uneven, and high above their water source, and they exhausted themselves searching for a place to lay their beds for the night. Without prompting, Roger volunteered to return to river level, using their newly notched pole, to bring them fresh water to quench their thirst. He returned with a full canvas pail of river water, and the party settled down eight hundred feet over Nude Canyon with a dark, cloudy sky delivering a light shower. By the time it was time to snuggle into their bedrolls in their modest alpine tent, the sky was clear and open.

Unfortunately, the cramped tent and relentless mosquitos allowed for only a fitful sleep. Assembling themselves the next morning was slow going, and it was not until a few minutes before 11:00 a.m. on June 15 that packs were shouldered and the crew moved out. The trail was distinctive in its rising and falling, sometimes with a change of several hundred feet in altitude.

The descent into Nude Canyon led them to a place to eat lunch, where the party noted the remains of a recent meal consisting of roasted goat; in Ferris Neave's estimation, it had been a repast of August Schnarr while checking his traplines. The right direction along the broken trail involved much guesswork, the only sign of previous passage among the winter windfall being the occasional notched pole ladder, at times buried in the edge of the river. The climbing party stopped for a rest at 5:00 p.m. above the Homathko River, with a view ahead of what Ferris Neave referred to as the "Great Canyon."[48]

A decision was reached to call this spot home for the night. Despite the sloped surface, Roger Neave took the initiative, and after the crew had hacked a level promontory with their ice axes on which to fix their tent and bedding, Roger softened the stony ground beneath their bedrolls with spruce boughs. Once they could relax somewhat, the crew took note, in the fading sun of the day and growing shadows, of the proliferation of ferns in this place, giving it the aspect of a place untouched previously by man or beast.[49]

The group got moving at 9:00 a.m. on the morning of June 16, dividing their forces. Arthur and Ferris looked after camp while Cam and Roger proceeded back to the notched ladder above Bellamy Creek. After the latter two had fished more items out of their cache there and lifted them to the top of the ladder, Arthur and Ferris picked them up to bring them to their advance camp among the ferns. This relay day would not end until 6:50 p.m.

The heavens opened up overnight, dampening the grounds and camping equipment and also creating a "general air of soddenness about tent-sack,"[50] Ferris Neave wrote in his diary. The next morning Roger took the initiative and got the Primus stove started, preparing a breakfast. Attempts to dry out their sacks and tents and clear debris from the rivulets of precipitation leading to their hastily cleared campsite were followed by an afternoon that cleared.

Departure came at 3:00 p.m. With a load of supplies and equipment in each of their packs, they descended into the Great Canyon, which brought them to a welcome clearing made from a small forest fire that appeared to have recently occurred. Higher ground revealed a landscape untouched by fire for a long time: a vast cedar stand and moss and lichen soft under their boots.

At this point, the men were eager to catch a glimpse through the trees of their objective, Mount Waddington, but their efforts were to no avail yet. They acknowledged the always-evolving nature of the terrain around them from one season to the next. As they began their descent, the route was interrupted where "a rock mass had recently broken away, leaving a vertical drop of some twenty feet."[51] Although the party was unsure of their route-finding abilities at this point, they used a double rope to descend the collapse in the trail, landing on a rocky, slaty outcropping where they fell into more doubt about which path to take. Roger pushed on ahead to reconnoitre and try to alleviate their confusion and frustration. Were they on the right trail? Proposals and counter-proposals ensued among the other three as they waited patiently for their leader to return. At last Roger's beaming face appeared, telling of possibility once again: One of the survey posts, most likely from 1928, was to be found at a point well below their present position. With renewed vigour the quartet continued, taking their own line downward and turning to the right, where a clear candidate for the night's campsite came into view. Even better, glittering in the trees below them was a landmark the climbing party knew about, Lowwa Lake, indicating that indeed they were on the right track. This was a place Don Munday had written about as being visible from the northwest peak in 1928.[52]

Also visible was the immense gorge of the Great Canyon. Ferris noted a tributary punished by flooding coming from the east that slunk its way into the Homathko, with another one joining the river farther along past the first one's forks. Again, the infrastructure created by previous travellers came in handy; on this occasion it was the raft Cam found already built on the south shore of Lowwa Lake.

Unfortunately, even though Munday had seen Lowwa Lake from Mount Waddington's northwest peak, the climbing party couldn't spot the northwest peak, or any bit of Waddington for that matter, from the shores of the lake. A cliff that presented an obstruction to their passage had clearly also presented an obstacle for an earlier party. Ferris wrote that the ready-made raft they found was perhaps the work, again, of trapper August Schnarr. At that point, the other climbers trusted their gear to the responsible Cam—he would use the raft to ferry the packs across to the west end of the lake—while the rest of them "scrambled across the cliffs."[53] Besides, once Cam had made up his mind, no one really wanted to disagree with him.

Each of the trio chose a slightly varying route as they climbed. Arthur went higher, and upon rejoining the Neave brothers he excitedly claimed that high peaks were visible to the west. Encouraged by this report, the men hurriedly tucked away their lunches before scrambling up to where Arthur had told of the sighting. The high point where they stood was ideally positioned between Lowwa Lake and the Homathko River for a glimpse of some of the major features on the approach to Mount Waddington. Most importantly, the men saw the prominent length of Tiedemann Glacier, the immense tongue of age-old ice that would be their route to their objective. This viewpoint struck a chord in Ferris, who wrote, "Of the three tremendous glaciers which radiate from the mountain, two, the Franklin and Scimitar, had so far not permitted parties to gain a footing on the higher, southeast peak. Tiedemann glacier might provide access to the east ridge or north face of this part of the mountain."[54]

From the viewpoint Arthur had led them to, the Neaves also could further glean their position as they could see the peaks southeast of Waddington, with Mount Munday at approximately 11,000 feet in elevation most likely in their sights. As they squinted farther, scanning the horizon to the west and noting the peaks like excited schoolboys, they took in views of Mount Merlon and Mount Marcus Smith, the latter named for the leader of the 1875 survey party whose infrastructure was helping them in their traverse. Among the many spires poking up in defiance of cloud cover, "Spearman Peak was easily recognized, though no mountaineer had seen it from this angle."[55] Ferris Neave scribbled in his diary, no doubt remembering the tales of his youth of first ascents in the Alps, "Exceedingly fine, buttresses of rock, snow + ice with Matterhorn-like summit."[56] Unfortunately, the cloud cover still obscured a clear view of their ultimate objective. "Billowing clouds lifting + sinking, revealed in glimpses wide snow saddle between Spearman Peak + Waddington," Ferris continued, seated on their promontory, his knees tucked in to create a platform for his notebook, "+ the pinnacled east ridge of W., the smaller lower pinnacle + the big upper one being visible at times."[57]

Straining to get a clear view of the true summit, the men now exulted in an ethereal world of their own, buoyed by many days of struggle in the Homathko River Valley, and now with seemingly little to obstruct them in achieving their goal of the true summit of Waddington. Clearly aware that they were the first mountaineers to spot the Mount Waddington district from this angle, Ferris continued to write furiously in his diary, attempting to capture the flavour, the nuance, the adjectives to define the moments of that first sighting. But the moment fell slightly short of expectations. Although their route was clear along "the huge mass of Tiedemann glacier curving gently to its snout" and beyond that features were clear such as icefalls and crags that introduced them to the landscape where their mettle would be tested, the sky up and to the right revealed only cloud. Like a watched pot that never boils, the men became impatient with the clouds, and it seemed to them that they waited a long time for the visual prize. Eventually the impenetrable cloud diffused, and through the lacy haze, they caught their first glimpses of "a great black ridge that seemed to sweep up into the sky." Sharp intakes of breath were followed by further pointing and interpretations. Although the final spire was never completely revealed, they "had momentary glimpses of the great pinnacles on the southeast ridge and of the slopes of snow and ice that sweep down toward Tiedemann glacier."[58]

It was not easy to turn themselves away from this reverie, this moment of adulation. They reached the mouth of Mosley Creek and found more infrastructure that the latest survey party to cross there had left behind and mostly intact. A bridge spanned the waterway across an intimidating, rocky gorge, although as Neave reported in his diary it was "a harrowing crossing, one of the 2 long logs being broken + the handrail obviously not intended for heavy-handed treatment."[59] Nevertheless, there were few options available, and the climbing party proceeded across, hopeful the bridge would hold up their weight, which included heavy packs of forty or fifty pounds. "It served our needs nobly," Ferris wrote in the CAJ, with a touch of his wit, "though in its present condition it does not inspire confidence in the mind of the timid, especially if the timid is heavily-packed."[60]

By 5:30 p.m. the men, now spent from their exhilarating day, found shelter above the boulders at the river. A bear's tracks were visible in the sand closer to camp on the south side of the water. Ferris noted, with much optimism after days of losing the trail, that the view from camp was familiar. In fact, it matched a woodcut engraving in his mind's eye. The engraving, called "Great Glacier, Bute Inlet," had been created by Frederick Whymper and appeared in his *Travel and Adventure in the Territory of Alaska, Formerly Russian America—now ceded to the United States—and in various other parts of the North Pacific*, published originally in 1869. "This is the place," Ferris wrote with a triumphant note, "from which Frederick Whymper sketched in 1864 the 'Great Glacier, Bute Inlet.'"[61] This was a suitable way to end a day in which three of them had seen glorious and optimistic sights, raising their morale from low and discouraged to spiritually uplifted. It was the "immense black mass" that had given Ferris encouragement when he had earlier studied the engraving and hoped it would prove to be the tower they wanted to ascend. Ferris tucked his pencil in his diary and pulled the elastic over the top to seal it.

On June 19, Ferris felt somewhat guilty about sleeping in until 7:45 a.m. The bounty of visual information from the day before had given the whole team the inspiration they needed to push onward. The foursome would resume their tramp through the woods, but first they had to retrieve their stuff from the last cache. After they had completed the caching relays, they went ahead at a brisk pace to Lowwa Lake.

It was 8:00 p.m. by the time they reached the shores. The heavens opened up and the rain poured. It was almost dark when they reached the raft that Cam had left and swiftly pushed off. The crew ate solemnly during the crossing of the lake, getting to the other side in an hour.

With Roger leading, they proceeded in the dark, unsure of their footing, as most surfaces were wet. Usually a lantern guided their way, but their source of light had run out of fuel while they travelled Tiedemann Creek. This was a real foil from the uplifting experience of sighting Waddington from the heights. The constant search for another campsite, the backtracking and relaying of their caches, and now physical troubles such as Arthur's blistered feet—all were signs that the party was becoming tired and beaten by the difficult terrain and weather conditions.

CHAPTER 6:

TIEDEMANN GLACIER

That physical and spiritual forces should exist in such close relationship in man when they are so essentially uncomplementary is, to my mind, the supreme miracle of creation. It is the infinite number of permutations and combinations, involved by the constant need to harmonize the physical and mental with the spiritual in relation to the complex forces of the universe, that affects our reactions to everything about us.

It is instinctive with man to investigate his relationship with the universe: he seeks truth, and on a mountain, when he is invigorated by physical exercise, pure air and the prospect before his eyes, his search is rewarded. Yet there are other occasions when the very forces that invigorate him and delight him conspire to render up beauty to ugliness and truth to falsehood.[1]

—F.S. Smythe, *The Spirit of the Hills*

Whereas the Neave expedition was taking the route along Tiedemann Glacier, the first attempt at Mount Waddington from
that approach, a northeastern approach had been made three
years earlier by Henry S. Hall Jr., a veteran of the Mount Logan expedition
of 1925. In contrast to the Neaves, Hall made the decision, in September 1931, to approach Mystery Mountain from along Mosley (locally
Homathko) Creek.[2] A year later Hall was back in the Waddington area,
having come from Bella Coola. He had brought Don Munday's published writings from the *Canadian Alpine Journal*'s earlier issues as well as
his detailed sketch map and photography. Looking down Scimitar Glacier to the west, Hall saw Monarch Mountain, known to be 11,712 feet.
Beyond Scimitar, Hall could see Mystery Mountain's neighbours. "Over
the end of the Scimitar glacier Mts. Geddes (right) and Bell (left), the latter
presenting an ice-clad east face, were prominent," Hall later wrote in the
Canadian Alpine Journal. "To the left of Mt. Tiedemann the peaks border-
ing Tiedemann Glacier: Mts. Asperity, Serra, Stiletto and Dentiform,
in order were easily made out. The whole massif has a characteristically
granitic profile and reminded me strongly of the aiguilles at Chamonix."[3]
With expert guide Hans Fuhrer by his side, Hall felt this alpine experience

to be reminiscent of an adventure in the Alps, and it generated some excitement between them. Routes from the northeast now seemed possible, and they talked about how to get at the peaks from there.

For Ferris Neave, who described the landscape ahead in his diary and compared it with the Matterhorn, how much would have Edward Whymper's first ascent of that seemingly unattainable peak been in his mind? Whymper *was* Victorian mountaineering. Despite the tragedy that took place on the descent in 1865, Whymper's description of the view from the summit had been the stuff of dreams for many an adventuresome lad. "There were the most rugged forms," Whymper wrote in *Scrambles Amongst the Alps*, "and the most graceful outlines—bold, perpendicular cliffs, and gentle undulating slopes; rocky mountains and snowy mountains, sombre and solemn, or glittering and white, with walls—turrets—pinnacles—pyramids—domes—cones—and spires! There was every combination that the world can give, and every contrast that the heart could desire."[4]

Such glory was nothing short of heavenly.

———•———

The climbing party had arrived at their camp at 10:45 the night before exhausted, soaked, and very hungry. Not surprisingly, they didn't rise until 10:40 the following morning, June 20. After eating brunch, they got underway at 2:15 p.m., proceeding west along the "bouldery flats." Here the landscape changed utterly as they reached "the huge debris-laden snout of Tiedemann Glacier."[5]

Ferris Neave wrote in the *Canadian Alpine Journal*, "The snout of Tiedemann glacier is buried beneath a chaotic jumble of moraine."[6] Up this moraine the group had to toil in order to cache their loads of supplies and equipment. Luckily the weather cooperated, with just a few cloudy periods. Unfortunately, in the distance Mount Waddington and the surrounding area were covered in cloud. They stopped at 5:15 p.m., found a sizeable rock on the moraine just to the left of the glacier itself, and stashed their goods. Finding the going easier on the descent, they arrived back at camp at 7:00 p.m., although Arthur Davidson was showing some wear, with a blister on one foot.

Although the heavens opened once more, Roger, ever the precocious engineer, designed a good oven using a "flake of rock + we had hot Tea – Bisk for late supper."[7] Ferris wrote about what they had learned from their initial climb the day before, taking advantage of "travelling up a lateral moraine which was a curiously thin dividing line between the sweet-smelling warmth of a thick spruce forest and the cold chaos of the great glacier."[8] Reaching the cache at the large rock at 12:20 p.m., they had lunch, then found an old lateral moraine that gave them a path "over stones + boulders, very slow + tedious." Their patience was to be rewarded from late afternoon on after they reached the open ice of the glacier, allowing for a good pace along a moderate grade and smooth surface. "Once we got past the terminal moraine," Roger recalled, "the glacier itself made a beautiful route up there. It was the gentlest sloping glacier with very few crevasses in the lower part."[9] Their camp on June 21 was on the left of their glacier path just past a grove of spruce on a patch of lateral moraine. Here Arthur spotted a goat, and the weather continued its dull, tepid showers. Ferris wrote in his diary, observing that Waddington in its heights appeared as a storm gathering, "wrapped in thick cloud + never visible."[10] It was Roger's birthday, and they broke out canned tomatoes and canned peaches as a treat.

After an overnight deluge the camp was soaked, and the crew did not get underway until 1:15 p.m. They descended for more cached gear. Arthur was now feeling his blistered foot more and he stayed behind on the ice, while Ferris, Roger, and Cam retrieved their goods at 4:00 p.m., turning around soon after.

The bad weather lifted, revealing new snow on nearby peaks. But because of the overnight rain, new "channels, runnels + pockets" had formed, deteriorating the conditions of the climb. Once they got to Arthur on the ice, they handed him his share of the cached load and proceeded back to the camp. In the clearing weather, the foursome got a dramatic glimpse not only of some of the heights of the Stiletto–Asperity Peaks but also of Mount Waddington in silhouette, with the sun setting on the other side.

Also, the day was notable for the men having spotted creatures that thrived in the moist, cool conditions of the glacier: various iceworms and collembola appeared on the surface of the glacier as it was refreezing.

These collembola—also called springtails or snow fleas—are arthropods that thrive in freezing temperatures.

They got back to camp at 9:25 p.m. in the fading light.

Ferris awoke to a tremendous view of Mount Waddington from his place in bed. Having awoken at 4:00 a.m., he managed to rouse himself and get a good look at the peak at daybreak through a telescope, the rising sun fully illuminating its eastern surfaces. "A magnificent picture," Ferris wrote in his diary on June 23, with only a few clouds presenting any kind of obscuration. This was all the encouragement he needed to proceed, the view giving him a psychological boost. The rest of the party had their boost from having seen a complete view of their silhouetted objective the evening before. "Its form from this side and distance," Ferris later wrote in the *Canadian Alpine Journal*, "is well-nigh perfect—massively buttressed at the base but with nothing of heaviness in its soaring height."[11]

The men had one more push to make before they could say they were at their launching point. The morning was spent organizing the collection of equipment and supplies they would cache there, then gathering the rest for placement on their backs for the move ahead, which began shortly before 1:30 p.m. With heavy packs carrying their necessities for the climb, the party reached the open ice of the glacier, leaving the moraine behind them. They were now in full view of Waddington and would be for the remainder of the day. Ferris took note of the lee of the glacier appearing "rather honeycombed and snow-like."

Chlamydomonas nivalis, also called snow algae, was visible again in the shade and in meltwater. This algae is crimson in appearance, and some climbers have compared it to blood. The sight of wriggling iceworms feeding on it can be startling, perhaps attributable to hallucination to those not aware of red snow and the glacier life it attracts.

A névé is a field of snow. It differs from a glacier in that it has no crevasses. Ferris noted reaching it by 4:00 p.m., and the team took this moment to rope up for the first time. This was common practice because despite the apparent ease of traversing a snowfield, there was no telling what lay beneath. Prominent member of the Alpine Club of Canada (former vice-president) and of the Revelstoke Mountaineering Club (former secretary-treasurer) J.P. Forde offered advice on using the rope in his article in the *Canadian Alpine Journal*. *The B.C. Mountaineer* republished it in installments for the benefit of its members.

> **Always use the rope when on a névé.** There is no exception to this rule. Snow may mask dangerous crevasses and yet may not be strong enough to carry a person. Crevasses are generally indicated by a slight concavity in the surface of the snow, which is of a somewhat darker shade than on the ice, but it is possible to overlook one, in which case one of the party may break through."[12]

They then stepped farther up the surface of the glacier, onto the névé, proceeding beyond the reach of timber, and found a place to camp on the north side of the flow of ice.

By 9:00 p.m. Ferris noted that an ice crust was starting to form on the meltwater. The climbers had noted storm clouds gathering far towards the east from where they had tramped. In his diary, Ferris further described the fine weather conditions where they were. "Magnificent view of range on opposite side of glacier," he noted. "Identified provisionally Mts. Marcus, Merlon, unnamed peak, Grenelle + Munday." Ferris also observed, further drawing on his guiding woodcut by Frederick Whymper, "Great Glacier, Bute Inlet," that from this location he could determine what might be the distinguishing geographic feature that had originally piqued his curiosity. "Whymper's 'black mass' is a shoulder of Grenelle." This feature, later marked as "Whymper Dome" on his hand-drawn map of the Coast Mountains, sits in a southern outcropping on the main body of Tiedemann Glacier, near a cluster of mountains.

The infectious desire to push on made it all the more difficult for Arthur to make a decision. What was a complaint about a blister had now developed into a failure of his footwear. Ferris wrote in his diary, "His boots are definitely unfit for much more work." Admittedly, Arthur was the least experienced mountaineer of the group. His boots were new on departure, and he had begun to show a lack of fortitude while following the rugged Homathko. "Arthur Davidson had not done much climbing before," Roger wrote. "His boots hadn't stood up to the trip down the Homathko valley very well."[13] According to Ferris, Davidson made a "cheerful" decision to remain behind at this camp, which they had determined would act as headquarters. From this point on, on June 24, no tent was going to be carried by the remaining trio, only "a single waterproof sleeping sack which we had designed, and Campbell had executed, during winter evenings in Winnipeg."[14] The mobile bed-for-the-night was a peculiar device, one intended specifically for life on snow. This homemade bit of ingenuity was another engineering triumph. As Ferris described it, "It just held the three of us and had enough room at the head end to allow us to sit up and still have a protective head flap over us. It required no pitching beyond throwing it down and unrolling it."[15]

"From base camp the three of us set off with food for eight days to attempt to make the climb," Roger told interviewer Susan Leslie in 1979. "We planned to carry everything possible to a high camp right on the col between Spearman Peak and the final summit of Mount Waddington."[16] The three-man sleeping bag, sometimes referred to as the tent sack, was heavy, however, making it difficult to lighten their load. "There was no lightweight down equipment in those days," Roger recalled later. "We also took of course a small stove with us."[17] Added to this were stove fuel, personal effects, and the photographic gear they needed to document their progress.

After the trio set out at 10:00 a.m. they made good progress across the névé despite the snow crust softening in the afternoon sun. Barring light cloud cover at times, they would get unobstructed glorious views of Waddington throughout the day. "Impressive views of Combatant, Tiedemann, Asperity, etc. in afternoon," Ferris noted, "but more cloud on them than on Waddington (wind from N.E.)."[18] They lunched on the open snowfield's expanse, and they would camp upon it that evening, calling it a day at 6:00 p.m. "We camped that night on the open glacier at the junction of a big tributary which owes its origin to the hanging glaciers of Mt. Munday, Spearman Peak and Mt. Waddington."[19] Throughout the afternoon, there was a proliferation of red snow and iceworms.

A cirque is a basin. Climbers can enter it through a gap from a glacier, but only where the basin is closed off on all other sides. Thus it is an enclosure, in this case leading to the men's objective, Mount Waddington. The cirque was closed off rather spectacularly. "As we went up

Tiedemann Glacier, when we got near the base of the peak the glacier became more crevassed," Roger Neave remembered. "Huge crevasses and this means quite a circuitous route to get around these crevasses. Sometimes crawling across rather flimsy-looking snow bridges."[20]

Once they had circumvented these obstacles, they trekked up towards the cirque of the glacier sourced by Mount Munday and Mount Waddington, nearly parallel with the Tiedemann Glacier. Ferris later wrote in his diary that he found this cirque "tremendously impressive, prob. at least 3000 ft. high at lowest point—a wall of ice + steep snow." Back at Lowwa Lake while getting a good view of the peaks, they had taken note of a prominent rock rib. It suggested a favourable route to the south, which was now to the left of their point of view as they approached the main objective via the saddle between Spearman Peak and Mount Waddington. But as the trio drew closer they saw the devil in the details. Ferris noted in the *Canadian Alpine Journal* that "it was evident that the whole of this part was swept at times by snow and ice avalanches from above. To the right [east] of the rib the going looked safer but there was the possibility of trouble with a big bergschrund some two thousand feet above us."[21]

A *bergschrund* is a gap, not unlike a crevasse but more complex. It is a large divide between a glacier's edge and the steep snow slope that has accumulated against the mountain's side. A bergschrund can be described at times as more of a chasm than a crevasse, and what was facing the Neave/Secord expedition was, potentially, a very challenging chasm. But first there was a network of crevasses to negotiate. To the south of a prominent rocky bluff they began to progress up a snow slope at a thirty-degree inclination. Roger took the lead, with the job of working out how to meander safely around these massive glaciers. The smooth névé of the day before was a memory.

> One [crevasse] which remains in the memory was spanned by a thin snow-bridge pierced by two holes through which the prone occupant got a stimulating view of the depths below. It was crossed by faith, eked out by a wriggling motion of the buttocks.

> Evening found us involved in a network of crevasses
> from which the only escape in an upward direction was
> by a direct assault on a very steep slope pounded hard
> by the passage of avalanches from above. We resolved
> not to tackle this till early morning. We threw down our
> bag, had supper in bed and waited until the first light
> showed over the peaks to the left of Tiedemann glacier.[22]

Although not announced explicitly in Ferris's diary or his account in
the *Canadian Alpine Journal*, this is where the trio began climbing the
peak they had come so far to attempt. Perhaps the mindful time spent
getting past crevasses took away some of the pomp and ceremony. Roger
Neave noted it: "And then we started to climb the actual peak," he said
simply. "We went up the Bravo Glacier, which is now the standard route
up Mount Waddington."[23]

Up until this point it was not necessary to use the crampons they had
brought with them, as the snow had been soft. But after they emerged
from the tent bag at 1:00 a.m., packed up, and ignited a lantern, they
put on their crampons in a pristine, clear world and Roger took the lead
again. Roger must have shown proficiency at this point, as it is usually
the best, most experienced climber who is roped into the lead position.
As J.P. Forde wrote in the *Canadian Alpine Journal*, in an article on
good climbing etiquette that had been reprinted across several issues of
The B.C. Mountaineer in 1927, the leader "should issue his orders firmly
and the others must obey him promptly, and cheerfully, even though
they may not be in perfect accord at all times."

> A disorganized party is always in danger, and when once
> the leader has decided on a certain course of action, his
> leadership must not be questioned. Of course, it is not
> intentioned that the other members of the party should
> be debarred from making a suggestion, or that the
> leader should be above accepting one, but when one is
> offered the matter of whether it is or is not to be acted
> upon must be left to the leader to decide. The position
> of the rest of the party is of minor importance, except
> one who has had experience, and who has a good bump

of locality, should be placed last, as he will be on the lead on the descent.[24]

Ideally, when it comes to intervals when on the rope, climbers are separated by equal distances except for the first and second climber, who should have more slack between them. In this case, the bowline would most likely have been applied to the last man, probably Cam, and the noose would have encircled the waist of the middle climber, Ferris. "It must always be remembered that if one climber slips nothing serious is likely to happen if every member of the party is doing his duty, while neglect of duty may have serious results," wrote J.P. Forde.[25]

They began with a steep slope. The pace was energetic, perhaps partly from enthusiasm and partly because they wanted to take advantage of the hard crust in the subzero temperatures. The sun was bound to heat things up as the morning wore on. The crampons helped them make the early morning as productive as possible. "The claws bit splendidly and saved us hours of step-cutting," Ferris later wrote.[26] Roger moved them efficiently up this steep slope before they went on to a relatively easy traverse across a wide uninterrupted snowfield in between crevasses. At that point, it was time to document where they were with a photograph looking out at Mount Munday. It was 4:45 a.m.

It was a view of superlatives, perhaps a reward for having negotiated all those crevasses. But a new adversary lay in wait: the bergschrund.

CHAPTER 7:

BERGSCHRUND

A bergschrund is nothing more than a glorified crevasse, one lip of which is considerably higher than the other. It is formed by a glacier moving away from the less tractable ice clinging to a mountain-side. A simple enough phenomenon, but one so necessary that one shudders to think what mountaineering would be like without it. Minus bergschrunds, it would be no more thrilling than modern Test-match cricket. What would the pioneers of the age have done without bergschrunds? How could the literature of the past have flourished without them? It would have been sadly reduced in its dramatic scope if this sort of thing did not intervene to lighten the account of a dull climb.[1]

—F.S. Smythe, *The Spirit of the Hills*

n *The B.C. Mountaineer*, in the May 1927 installment of the serialized article "Hints on the Use of the Rope in Mountain Climbing," J.P. Forde quoted the late A.F. Mummery, mountaineer author of *My Climbs in the Alps and Caucasus* and influential proponent of guideless climbing: "Among the mountains, as elsewhere, 'the unexpected always happens.' It is the momentary carelessness in easy places, the lapsed attention, or the wandering look that is the usual parent of disaster. The first lesson the novice has to learn is to be always on his guard, and it is one the oldest climber rarely fully masters."[2]

The trio now approached a significant split in the ice-scape, separating two plates of ice. The bergschrund was a deep cut, marking a place of decision. Ferris wrote later that they "emerged on a level step below the bergschrund. Much to our relief, the latter was bridged by a vertical mass of ice, up which Roger cut a way to the snow above."[3]

Roger's 1979 interview recollections of the days at this point in their climb were more of an overview, one in which he may have seen the bergschrund as a very large crevasse, but also where he remembers the progress made as a series of camps. "We camped once at the base of the peak. We camped once partway up the Bravo Glacier, and then from the top of the

Bravo Glacier we climbed an extremely steep snow slope: 48 degrees measured by clinometer."[4] The previous days' route through the icefall's large crevasses had proved to be a challenge; an upcoming snow-slope bridge, immense and awkwardly constructed, would prove even more difficult. Roger led the trek up the delicate bridge, which would be their route across the definitive split. The bridge was nearly vertical, requiring Roger to cut steps for Ferris and Cam. "R. had arduous time—snow still hardish," Ferris later wrote in his diary. He later also tried to describe the crossing of the bergschrund in a diary entry in which the men "packed out a route across + above bergschrund which we were approaching. Crossed latter by large + chaotic bridge (5:30) + up 250 ft. snow slope (48°) to rocks (6:30)."[5]

The geology at this height was peculiar—all rocks tilted to the right. A slim snow arête appeared, taking them to Spearman Saddle, a place in the snow just under Waddington Col. It was at this point their luck ran out. Under the weight of their forty-pound packs, the crust finally gave way. Their legs plunged in up to their knees, making each step more of an effort. "The snow was now softening in the glare of another brilliant day, and we traversed along the snow-covered rocks to the right," Ferris later wrote.[6] He called the snow "execrable." The sun seemed to penetrate everything now, searing through the thin ice surface layer, causing them to perspire. In such a steep snow slope, with softening snow, the climbers' practice was simple. In order to maintain a position on the mountain, J.P. Forde advised in the 1927 republication of his article:

> **When ascending or descending a steep snow slope, pass a loop of the rope around the handle of your ice axe and stick the point of the handle hard into the snow at every step.** The friction of the rope around the handle will greatly assist in arresting the progress of anyone who slips.[7]

If melting snow crust was not enough, they were about to meet up with a massive and unexpected obstacle. "Just as we breasted the top we were confronted by an enormous crevasse which ran the whole width of the slope from the cliffs of Spearman Peak to the steep edge on our right," Ferris wrote.[8] Traipsing along, searching for a way across, they noticed a naturally constructed bridge. Although deemed "flimsy" by Ferris, he felt it just might hold their individual weights and get them across the chasm.

When it comes to snow and ice bridges, the words of J.P. Forde republished by the B.C. Mountaineering Club are quite clear:

> **Never allow more than one party on a doubtful snow bridge at the same time.** If this rule is observed there is only a chance of one breaking through, and this chance is much less than if more than one are on it.

> **Never jump on a snow bridge.** Cross it as carefully as possible, so as not to jar it. There may be others to follow you and you may need it on your return.[9]

They persevered, bridging the enormous bergschrund by way of the frail bridge, which Roger carefully crawled across on his hands and knees, followed by Ferris and Cam. If they fell accidentally, they would land on a steep snow slope and slide deep into the bergschrund. Luckily, they were inching their way across it while it was still late morning. Crossing a snow bridge in the heat of the afternoon would be deadly, although the sun of the late morning was already causing snowmelt.

> **Remember that snow bridges are likely to be much weaker in the afternoon than in the morning.** The cold during the night will have tightened them up by morning. But the morning sun will have weakened them by noon. Therefore, it is not safe to assume that because a bridge carried you in the morning it will carry you in the afternoon.[10]

Upon standing up in knee-deep snow, the trio took stock of their surroundings. This anxiety-ridden crossing had brought them to 10,000 feet. They were now firmly in between Spearman Peak and the sharp, prominent shoulder that forms the northeast buttress of Mount Waddington. Before them, gleaming in the sunlight, appeared the nemesis of Don and Phyllis Munday, an ineffable presence at first, and then to the Neave brothers and Cam Secord a truly nightmarish blade: the final peak.

After their trying morning that had begun in the wee hours, they had a well-deserved meal; the food would do them good after many burned calories on the steep climb. Then they brought out their socks for drying in the sun and threw down the tent sack, eager to rest. They also preferred to pass the rest of the warm afternoon away from the potential of a dangerous passage across the melting ice and snow. As J.P. Forde prescribed:

> **Eat and drink as much as possible when climbing.** This is necessary to prevent your vitality from becoming low and should be done even if you have to force yourself to do it. The drink should NOT be ice water.[11]

Roger recalled that their hard morning's work had its rewards. After another meal at 8:30 p.m., they lessened the weight of their packs by leaving some food and gear behind, then continued on their way up "and got onto a rock rib that eventually let us onto the snow slopes above and from there it was comparatively easy going up between the col between Spearman Peak and Mt. Waddington, which is where we made our next camp that night." Despite the fragile snow crust, they were keen to make progress, and they moved up, with Cam leading. They encountered some very large crevasses once again but circumvented the obstacles by taking the bridges across to the west. The snow's surface couldn't hold their weight and their legs kept sinking in up to their knees or higher, with each step more arduous and exhausting. The heat of the day caused enough melt that it would be overnight before the crust was again hard and thick enough to allow for easier going.

> **Everyone should look after and be responsible for the portion of the rope between himself and the man ahead.** This will place a definite duty on each one and will leave the leader free to select the best course and pick out good hand and foot holds.[12]

Cam's long-legged gait was suited for the snow conditions, with the men still puncturing through the thin ice after the heat of the day. They were "using Campbell's long legs to take the first soundings in the horribly-yielding snow."[13] They stopped, bathing in the moon's rays at

10:30 p.m. at a point below Spearman Saddle. Taking in their surroundings before turning in, they could make out the peaks to the northeast —Combatant, Tiedemann, and Asperity—which appeared much nearer, "Combatant taking pride of place for the beauty of its gothic form. . . . We camped in the snow just under the crest of the col—a spot we referred to as Spearman saddle. With a camp established at 10,500 feet and food for at least three days the prospects looked fair indeed. The weather was still good but patches of light fog at the col and a slight clouding in the east made us a little anxious."[14]

The men turned into their tent sack at 11:00 p.m. The ice-encased final spire oversaw all in the moonlight.

———•———

"The weather so far had been beautiful. Cloudless and sunny and warm," Roger Neave recalled years later. "But when we woke up early the next morning, the picture was completely changed. It was snowing, clouds were down, we couldn't see any more than a few feet from the tent ... from the sleeping bag, I should say!"[15] After this reflective statement in 1979, Roger let out a little chuckle. But most likely when the trio looked around beyond the hood of their homemade tent sack, they were not laughing.

All the same, it was 2:00 a.m. on June 27 and time to rise. The three men hurriedly put on the boots they'd brought into the tent sack the night before in an effort to keep the footwear from freezing. Roger pumped the Primus and ignited it to life. The flame coming from the stove's base was an alien sight in the dank cloud that surrounded them, a dim bit of illumination. But Ferris could see daylight coming from the east along their path in Tiedemann Valley, which gave them glimmers of hope. By the time they'd had a little breakfast, at 3:00 a.m. the temperature was at -4°C. Their hopes faded with the light from the east as the cloud cover thickened around them, "and we could not see even the big séracs a few yards from our camp," Ferris wrote, referring to the unstable ice towers nearby.[16] J.P. Forde advised:

> **Never attempt a difficult climb except when the mountain is in good condition.** It's always bad during a storm and for at least two days after.

> **Never attempt a climb in bad weather.** And if a storm
> should come on, even threaten during a climb, turn back
> at once and get to safe ground as quickly as possible.[17]

This was from a playbook of common knowledge that all three of them knew very well. Considering how far they had all come and the encouragement from the previous day's progress, this was a heavy blow indeed.

During his 1979 interview, Roger Neave brought up what they were no doubt thinking at the time. "It was just impossible to go anywhere, the way the clouds were, you couldn't find your way anywhere."[18] By 9:00 a.m. snow was falling hard and visibility was only a few yards. The temperature dropped to –28°C. "Could scarcely distinguish up from down," Ferris later scribbled in his diary. "Retired to the tent sack + remained there during the day, eating light meals *in situ* at 9.00 + 2.00."[19] They could only be patient and wait in their homemade sleeping bag.

The cloud weighed heavy. The snow fell silently. They were in two cocoons—the tent sack and a light grey world around them. Perhaps they were grasping at straws, but by late afternoon, they spied light, which turned into a sudden clearing. By 4:45 p.m. they had had enough of waiting and emerged from the sack with the intent of climbing all night, despite their better judgement. It was a full moon that night, so they'd have as much illumination as possible. It was now or never. Perhaps this would also help them somehow. They roped up and Roger led off. It was 5:00 p.m.

Initially it was hard to get their bearings. All they could do was stand. Looking south through cloud, they could just make out a glacier and peaks. As they struggled in snow that, despite the cold, had them breaking through the crust to their knees, they made use of their clinometer. They could at least determine that they were above the height of Spearman Peak at 11,000 feet. Mount Munday was out there somewhere to the southeast at 11,400 feet, and they determined they were at least at that height. Despite this progress, it was difficult to note their accomplishment as the earlier weather conditions returned. Roger handed the lead over to Ferris. "Then the clouds came down again and visibility was reduced to a few feet."[20] They made progress slowly through the driving snow, but they couldn't see. Over and over, Ferris drove his ice axe to the hilt into the snow. The slope became steeper, reaching an incline of thirty-eight degrees. Finally, there was some reprieve as they reached a level patch of snow. What they couldn't determine at the time was that they were close to the base of the final tower.

In the driving snow, a decision had to be made. A quick conference took place, the three shouting over the snow and wind. A decision was unanimous. In this lost state, without any sign of improvement, climbing any farther would be extremely dangerous. Even if they proceeded and achieved success atop the final tower, it would most likely be a one-way trip. This was not reasonable. At 8:00 p.m. the trio reluctantly turned back. Roger took the lead from Ferris. Their earlier steps were still lightly visible impressions, and they followed those breadcrumbs back to the tent sack, which took just over an hour. Roger got the stove ignited as the skies darkened. They ate a silent meal in the gloom. Then they all piled into the tent sack, which was sodden but to their relief provided some warmth. They had most likely reached the 12,000-foot mark that day, but it was hard to tell for sure.

"The third day," Roger recalled, "the weather still was not good, but it looked as if it might possibly break, so we set out again and got to the base of the final tower."[21] But the early morning of June 28 did not present ideal climbing conditions. They were still "enveloped in cloud with squalls of fine new snow sweeping towards the col," and it appeared they would have another spotty day where climbing would be a game of chance. If anything, it was the soggy tent sack that got them going— they did not want to face any more time stuck in there. Ferris later justified their decision to try again, writing, "A sickly sun could be made out overhead and the pinnacles and final tower could be studied during our advance."[22]

J.P. Forde wrote:

> **Take an extra supply of food with you.** You may be detained beyond the expected time, and hunger does not add to the delights of a night spent on a mountain.[23]

There was a conspiracy of silence among them. They knew they did not have enough food, despite having packed for a contingency such as what they were experiencing. "This was the last day we could climb,"

Roger admitted later. "The weather was still not good. But it did give us enough encouragement that we kept on going."[24]

They climbed on in the grey world, knowing that the trek would become even more challenging and that they would have to switch to rock climbing before long in the treacherous conditions. "We got to the base of the final rock tower," Roger recalled. It was 10:05 a.m., and they "had reached the end of last night's track." He added, "We tried to get over to our snow slope on the east side which went up quite high."[25] What they encountered was another massive bergschrund, this one about sixty feet high. The trio could find no way to cross it. No snow bridge presented itself except a distant span to the west, and with the men still plunging into the soft snow to their knees, the physical expenditure was something they couldn't justify. They turned back to the rock tower's base, where they ate a quick lunch. Trying again from there, they found a way up, with leader Roger cutting steps up fifteen feet to a projection of rock. After that, another one hundred and fifty feet of steps had to cut, which took an hour and a half, and by then it was 2:00 p.m.

After the steps, they gained purchase on rocks at last, traversing a snowy ledge. With the final tower looking down on them, still encased in ice and much new-fallen snow, the trio went up a steep pitch before taking a diagonal route to the west. The steeper rock incline and the greater elevation combined with new snow falling created almost impossible climbing conditions, which they were well aware of, the mountain having received snowstorms for at least two days now. "Worked up + across several hundred feet, very slow, R. leading very skillfully + painstakingly," Ferris later wrote in his diary.[26] In retrospect, reflecting on their dire situation, he wrote the following in the *Canadian Alpine Journal*:

> From this point we worked slowly upward and westward about parallel with the edge of the snow-slope which lies on the northwest side of the rock tower. The latter is everywhere exceedingly steep and the small ledges were plastered with ice and piled with new snow—with more coming. Almost every hold had to be chipped out or scraped before use and only the painstaking work of our leader and great care on the part of all of us,

prevented certain parts of the route from being unreasonably dangerous. We climbed throughout with mitts, ropes and straps frozen to the consistency of boards.[27]

At 6:00 p.m., the Neave/Secord effort to climb the final tower was aborted. The weather was "impossible." They were on the northwest tower, highly exposed, four hundred feet above where they had achieved the projection of rock. They stopped climbing about eight hundred feet from the summit of the final spire.

"We decided we couldn't go down the way the way we'd come up," Roger recalled. "It was too hazardous. So we put in a piton and rappelled down, with a rope through it and rappelled down eighty feet."[28]

Ferris's assessment of their decision to not use their route up on the way back down was in agreement with Roger's. "Looking back along our line of ascent it now seemed frankly inconceivable that any human being would have attempted it."[29]

In getting down to the bergschrund, they also had to rappel another section. Roger put in another piton, and they rappelled to a point where that morning they had attempted to get up on top of the snow slope. "The snow slope was very steep and not too solid," Roger noted years later. "We were afraid that it might avalanche."[30] They did not want to waste any more time on this unstable slope. The last of the day's light had bled away, and although they knew they were near the massive bergschrund, they had no way to determine this with their eyes.

Suddenly, part of the roof of the bergschrund collapsed under Ferris's weight. It was only the section of the "upper lip" that was under his foot, but even so it set up a reverberation that was felt by other members of the climbing party. "The vibration which this disturbance set up was felt distinctly by Roger, who was now the last man on the rope, but nothing more fell."[31] Nevertheless, this was a clear threat. All three men drove their ice axes into the snow. With the wind howling around them, they shouted at each other about what to do next. Roger suggested lowering a rucksack down. Ferris and Cam readily agreed. The rucksack was lowered and touched bottom in ten feet. With much doubt about whether the surface they were standing on would hold, they next lowered Cam down into the darkness. He shouted up that he was on the ledge, in the company of the rucksack, and nearby was a shelter: a cave! It was a hollowing out of the ice-wall. With a look at each other the brothers crept down the ten feet, guided by the illumination of a lantern, and reunited with Cam. Although they still could feel the howling wind and blowing snow, they looked around the shelter. "Cave was very long with icicles, ice lumps, snow banks, etc.," Ferris wrote in his diary. Surrounding them "was a great irregular cavern with fantastic pillars and friezes on the walls," Ferris wrote. This appeared to be the structure of their deliverance. "Every few minutes a wild blast of air laden with fine snow particles swept in through the entrance."[32] A snowbank had been created as a result, and they carved a deeper shelter in it so they could avoid the freezing wind and the snow blowing in.

Roger lit the Primus stove. Although they were protected from the exposure outside the cave, it was still bitterly cold. The alternative was beyond thinking about. They would wait out the blizzard outside in this fantastical structure. Roger reported later that "Campbell got his toes slightly frozen," but even so, they could make hot drinks with the Primus. Ferris was impressed by how, even in the nook they'd carved out for the little stove, the snow never melted around it.

By 3:00 a.m. light appeared through the entrance. They knew they were in for a rough return to Arthur Davidson. But there was no doubt that the cave of pillars and friezes had sheltered them from the worst of the blizzard. Although the storm continued, they were on the right path: Further climbing up the final peak would have been a death sentence.

Playing cat and mouse with crevasses, traversing the glacier that had guided them west to the land of superlatives, eventually brought them down to the jumble of the moraine. "The weather was now improving rapidly and before we reached Arthur's camp in the afternoon Waddington was clear again," Ferris later wrote, "though whiter than we had yet seen it."[33] The diary entries fall short of providing the reader with a glimpse of the men's thoughts and feelings in having achieved the heights they did. Perhaps this was due to the stoicism of the time. The diary was a record of the expedition, presented objectively. Technically, the climb was a failure. But the mountaineering community would see this attempt from the east, from the far-off foundry of the Canadian mountaineering community, Winnipeg, as being nothing short of remarkable, and their accomplishment would increase the draw of this remarkable mountain.

Looking east down Tiedemann Glacier from Waddington's Snow Peak.

CHAPTER 8:

DEATH ON THE SOUTHEAST RIDGE

Mr. Hadow slipped, fell against him, and knocked him over. I heard one startled exclamation from Croz, then saw him and Mr. Hadow flying downwards; in another moment Hudson was dragged from his steps, and Lord Francis Douglas immediately after him. All this was the work of a moment. Immediately we heard Croz's exclamation, old Peter and I planted ourselves as firmly as the rocks would permit: the rope was taut between us, and the jerk came on us both as on one man. We held; but the rope broke midway between Taugwalder and Lord Francis Douglas. For a few seconds we saw our unfortunate companions sliding downwards on their backs, and spreading out their hands, endeavouring to save themselves. They passed from our sight uninjured, disappeared one by one, and fell from precipice to precipice on the Matterhorn below, a distance of nearly 4,000 feet in height. From the moment the rope broke it was impossible to help them.[1]

—Edward Whymper, "Descent of the Matterhorn"

After the disaster that befell those four men after that first ascent of the Matterhorn in 1865, Edward Whymper, along with "old" Peter Taugwalder and his son "young Peter," remained immobile for a half hour. Whymper was stunned, and both old and young Taugwalder, according to Whymper's written account, were "paralysed with terror, cried like infants, and trembled in such a manner as to threaten us with the fate of the others."[2]

In time, the trio made the descent towards Zermatt, but it was trying and fraught with terror. At the point when much of the difficulty was over, at the descending ridge towards the town, the group remembered the fallen climbers and began to bellow their names over the ridge in hopes of receiving a reply. There was nothing heard in return. Silent and crestfallen, they solemnly continued the descent. It was at this point that Whymper noted a sight that he could not explain.

> When, lo! a mighty arch appeared, rising above the Lyskamm, high into the sky. Pale, colourless, and noiseless, but perfectly sharp and defined, except where it was lost in the clouds, this unearthly apparition seemed like

a vision from another world; and, almost appalled, we watched with amazement the gradual development of two vast crosses, one on either side. If the Taugwalders had not been the first to perceive it, I should have doubted my senses. They thought it had some connection with the accident, and I, after a while, that might bear some relation to ourselves. But our movements had no effect upon it. The spectral forms remained motionless. It was a fearful and wonderful sight; unique in my experience, and impressive beyond description, coming at such a moment.[3]

Edward Whymper's tone in *Scrambles Amongst the Alps* in describing the tragedy on the descent from the Matterhorn in 1865 is stoic but uncharacteristic of him. He was perhaps challenged when he wrote the chronology of events, not only because of the difficult experience described but also because of the helplessness he experienced when the tragedy occurred. These men had fallen in their prime, immediately following a moment of extraordinary spiritual enlightenment, into the void. Perhaps Whymper also felt a responsibility to those who might later try to climb the monarch of the Alps. However, the apparition can only be placed in the realm of the unexplained.

————•————

Unbeknownst to the Neave expedition up Waddington in 1934, another attempt was being made on the final tower, this one from the west. Alec Dalgleish, Alan Lambert, Eric Brooks, and Neal M. Carter had met at Glendale Cannery at Knight Inlet on June 18, while the Neave expedition was at Lowwa Lake. The Dalgleish expedition would meet with disaster, as Carter later wrote in the *Canadian Alpine Journal*: "The fatal accident which befell Alec Dalgleish while essaying the ascent of Mt. Waddington (13,260 ft.), highest peak in the Coast range of British Columbia, was one of those tragic happenings which take place with such despairing suddenness that little opportunity for ascertaining the causes presents itself."[4]

In his sonorous voice, Dr. Neal M. Carter introduced Phyllis Munday's 1964 oral presentation recording, "Old Ways to Waddington." In it, he pays homage to and indicates his own following of the Mundays' explorations in the Coast Range and their regular expeditions in the 1920s and 1930s to Mystery Mountain, later Mount Waddington. "Phyl Munday, and her late husband Don, accomplished what may well be termed, the foremost mountaineering epic in the southern part of the British Columbia coast mountains, namely, the identification of the highest mountain completely within the province, and the first exploration of the unmapped stupendous array of peaks and glaciers immediately surrounding it."[5]

Carter launches into a brief presentation of historical data of the region, including information about the 1875 Canadian Pacific Railway survey party led by Marcus Smith. But he also acknowledges, in the terminology of his time, the First Nations' use of the land long before mountaineers began tramping the hills. "Native Indians of British Columbia are known to have used the valley of the Homathko river as a travel route between the head of Bute Inlet and the Interior long before the advent of the white man," Carter said. "They were still using it until the end of the 1880s."[6]

His warm introduction is punctuated with moments where he recalls his affiliation with Phyl and Don Munday. Some of the stories were adventurous, others sombre, such as in 1947 when he accompanied Don into the Waddington area to retrieve the body of an American climber. This was Don Munday's final trip into the area he had helped to make so famous.

Carter goes on to explain his further connection with the Mundays, especially through their mutual involvement in the BCMC: "I first met Don and Phyl Munday in the British Columbia Mountaineering Club about a month after their marriage in 1920. During succeeding years, I was on many an enjoyable trip with them, but never had the opportunity of accompanying them on any of their dozen or so trips to the Waddington area which commenced with their first exploratory approach in 1925."[7]

Early on in his involvement with the BCMC, Carter became editor of *The B.C. Mountaineer*, during the time in which the Mundays were making their preliminary sorties into the Coast Range in the mid-1920s. As such, he would have seen the growing momentum of the mountaineering community in Vancouver. As Canadian mountaineering historian Chic Scott puts it:

During the 1930s Vancouver was the centre of a very active climbing community. Much of the activity was promoted by the two local climbing clubs, the BCMC and the Vancouver Section of the Alpine Club of Canada. Vancouver mountaineers normally climbed on peaks close to the city, but a few bold souls ventured farther north into the great wilderness that was being opened up and ardently described by the Mundays and Henry Hall. Chief among these adventurers was Tom Fyles who had been a leading member of the BCMC for almost twenty years. He was joined by three younger men: Neal M. Carter, who had been climbing since age fourteen and was both talented and experienced; Mills Winram, a student in agricultural economics at UBC; and Alec Dalgleish, a budding artist and a passionate rock climber.[8]

In the spring of 1926, Carter took over the role of editor of *The B.C. Mountaineer* from H.D. Foster. This ideally positioned him to be aware and informed of current mountaineering activities, as well as to chronicle the various Munday expeditions in the direction of Mystery Mountain. In his first editorial, he not only pointed out the important roles the B.C. Mountaineering Club and *The B.C. Mountaineer* were playing in the development of alpinism, but also demonstrated how his sense of humour would factor into his writing.

> At the beginning of the fourth year of publication it is not out of the way to recall the purpose of this publication, with first a brief word of appreciation to Messrs. Munday and Foster who piloted it through the difficult early years. There are many criticisms made. Of course! This is natural and desirable for it shows the interest of the members; but when criticizing, reflect on what your course would be if you were in charge.
>
> Most members say: "Make the Bulletin more readable," but entertainment is not the main purpose we have.

We must first print official notices and information. These are ephemeral and should be as short as possible. The important thing is the record of mountaineering endeavor, which, because of lack of space, must be condensed, and condensed information is no more palatable than condensed milk; but it must be there so that ten years hence a party can plan a trip solely on the information published this year. Then, and only then, if space remains, we can regale you on stories of maidens leaving their boots in a crack in the rock, or hornet-maddened ponies strewing the trail with our belongings —with this reservation, that many do not appreciate the relation of such incidents when they themselves are concerned, and we cannot tread on tender toes.[9]

In a brief clipping in the June 1926 issue, Carter brought out the efforts of Phyl and Don Munday in the context of the prominent northern mountaineering expedition the previous year.

Mr. and Mrs. Don Munday, supported by Mr. T.H. Ingram and others, are emulating the success which crowned the efforts to conquer Canada's highest peak, Mt. Logan, by making an expedition to what may prove "to be the highest point in all this province." Considering the fact that part of the summit of Mt. Fairweather, 15,400 feet, lies in this province, this new "mystery mountain" must indeed be a giant.

It was first seen by Mr. and Mrs. Munday from Mt. Arrowsmith, and later from a summit above the head of Bute Inlet, last year. Apparently lying in the unmapped district surrounding Chilco Lake, its inaccessibility will probably cause the party to be gone a month.[10]

Could Neal Carter have been already taking notes, dreaming of joining the Mundays on their forays into the unknown? He certainly was encouraged to develop his own understanding of the Coast Mountains closer to home. "In the early 1920s he made several first ascents in Garibaldi Park," Chic Scott wrote, "and carried out the first survey that resulted in the first topographic map of the park. He climbed extensively in the Tantalus Range and also made the first topographic map of that area."[11]

In the July 1926 issue of *The B.C. Mountaineer*, as editor Carter penned a front-page article about the summer camp planned for the following summer days in the "alpine wonderland" on the Black Tusk Meadows of Garibaldi Park. "The Bell-Irving Camp is being immediately followed by the BCMC Camp," Carter wrote, "the dates for the former being July 14th to August 7th, and for the latter, Aug. 8th to Aug. 22nd." Much of the article was spent encouraging members to sign up sooner rather than later, to avoid disappointment in attending the climbing event in a park that was a point of interest for him. "On their return, glowing accounts of the trips and adventures at the camp will doubtless fire many of our new members and their friends with the enthusiasm and desire of seeing the Park for themselves," Carter wrote with his own thinly veiled enthusiasm for the climbing venue.[12] But on the next page, Carter had placed a brief blurb at the top left pointing out the return of the Mundays from the forbidding lands to the north, and also enticing the reader with further tales of courage and reconnaissance from the land of the mysterious mountain. "Although unsuccessful in attaining the summit of the high peak which formed the object of a five-weeks' trip to the country west of Chilco lake, Mr. and Mrs. Don Munday and party have returned with much interesting information regarding the wonderfully glaciated area surrounding this peak. The full report of the expedition is anticipated with great pleasure."[13]

Carter's keenness for knowledge of Mystery Mountain was already beginning to show. But he was also part of the growing momentum that would lead to an increasing number of expeditions into the Waddington area. By the mid-1930s, snippits had turned to multi-issue chronicles, and the demand from regional mountaineers to read about this growing movement matched the increase in traffic into the region itself. Mountaineers were gathering with increasing enthusiasm, and Neal Carter was certainly in line for his own attempt on Waddington. "In the 1930s, in the company of Alec Dalgleish and Tom Fyles, [Carter] explored the peaks at the head of the Toba and Lillooet rivers," wrote historian Chic Scott. "In 1934 he was a member of the Vancouver team attempting Mount Waddington when Alec Dalgleish was killed."[14]

Alec Dalgleish was twenty-six when he died. Not unlike Campbell Secord, he was already an accomplished rock climber. Scottish-born, he moved to Canada while young, living in Calgary, then Vancouver. He had an interest in photography. By this time, Phyllis Munday was the honorary photographic secretary for the Alpine Club of Canada and a mountaineering photographer to which to aspire.

From 1932 to 1934, the year of his death, Dalgleish was a student at the British Columbia College of Arts, studying under Jock Macdonald and Fred Varley. He showed promise in both art and mountaineering, and with his rock-climbing prowess he was seen as a contender to make quick work of the final tower of Waddington.

He was also a promising writer, with an article titled "The Source of the Toba River" featured in the 1934 *Canadian Alpine Journal*, vol. XXII.[15] But the feature article lineup in the 1934 issue of the *CAJ* was dominated by two Coast Mountain starters by Don Munday, followed by articles by Ferris Neave and Neal M. Carter, the latter reporting on "The Fatal Accident on Mt. Waddington." Dalgleish's obituary topped the In Memoriam section, followed by that of legendary Austrian guide Conrad Kain.

The previous year, on July 8, 1933, Dalgleish, Neal M. Carter, Tom Fyles, and Mills Winram boarded the SS *Chelohsin*, the stalwart steamship that had brought the Mundays up to Bute Inlet in their early Mystery Mountain expeditions. They changed to a smaller gas boat and motored up into the glacial-silt blue waters of Toba Inlet, then when the tides were in their favour, up the Toba River Valley. A highlight of their adventure for Dalgleish was climbing, on July 15, to the height of 9,150 feet atop Julian Peak. The view during their climb was remarkable.

> Many previously unseen peaks were now visible to the north and west while a few miles away, between us and the north branch of the Toba River rose a heavily glaciated summit, apparently higher than the one on which we stood. Much farther in the same direction (northwest) were two outstanding masses. These were

> probably Raleigh and Gilbert, 10,100 and 10,200 feet,
> shown on the recently published four-sheet map of
> B.C., and located on the watershed of the Bishop River,
> a tributary of the Southgate. Still further to the north-
> west, Mts. Waddington and Tiedemann could be seen.[16]

In the period between the adventure up the Toba River Valley in 1933 and the publication of "The Source of the Toba River" in the *CAJ* a year later, Dalgleish met his fate, and his friend and fellow climber Neal Carter left a footnote at the bottom of the initial page of the article. "Owing to the tragic accident which befell the writer of this article the year following the expedition herein reported, it has been suggested that a revision of certain place names mentioned in the article and sketch map be made. It would seem appropriate that Julian peak be re-named Mt. Dalgleish, and the name Julian peak be transferred to the peak marked '5' on the sketch map. —N.M.C."[17]

During their expedition up Toba River in 1933, perhaps while ascending the peak that was fated to be named after him, Dalgleish had discerned Mount Waddington in the distance and had expressed his desire to climb to the top of the gleaming peak. The plans were struck: They would try it the following summer, going after the final peak from the southeast. Joining them would be Alan Lambert and Eric Brooks. Lambert and Dalgleish, both members of the B.C. Mountaineering Club, would organize the event over the winter. Dalgleish, Carter, and Brooks were also members of the Alpine Club of Canada.

"The party met June 18th at Glendale Cannery, Knight inlet, and continued to the beach just north of the mouth of the Franklin river near the head of the inlet. Eighteen days were to elapse before the boat was to expect the return of the party to the beach and since the weather was doubtful, it was decided to take things easy and [relay] the packs to the proposed base camp at Icefall point instead of attempting to [make] one [camp] through trip[s] with very heavy loads."[18] They "established Base Camp at Icefall Point along the Franklin Glacier on June 23."[19]

In the following days, Mount Waddington was studied and short sorties were made into the Repose Glacier, traversing Franklin Glacier to the east and the ridge behind their base camp. Carter described a full moon rising in a cloudless sky. They traversed Corridor Glacier and rounded the base of Jester Mountain, then reached the base of Waddington. "A steep, 600-foot snow gully giving access to a buttress joining the main ridge about half-way between the peak and the Waddington-Spearman pass was selected for the first attempt."[20] Although this buttress was steep, the going proved to be good, and without any wind weather conditions were about as ideal as could be. Carter took pains to establish that the ropes used were of good standard, although one had seen more climbs than the other. Lambert and Dalgleish were alternating the responsibility of taking the lead. "Progress was quite slow with only one person advancing at a time, secured by belaying or holding of the rope from above," Carter wrote. Within the pages of a recent issue of *The B.C. Mountaineer* was spelled out the proper procedure in placing the climbing party at proper intervals on the rope: "These intervals should be equi-distant, except in the case of that between the leader and the second man, which should be a few feet greater than the rest. This will often afford him a better opportunity of selecting safe anchorages from which to assist the ascent of the other members in the party. What the exact length of the intervals should be varies according to the nature of the climbing to be encountered, and no definite distance can be laid down for it."[21]

"Vantage points for assistance became less frequent," Carter later wrote, "and it became necessary to change the spacing of the rope intervals in order to give Dalgleish more scope for upward exploration before advancing to the next stop."[22] Dalgleish had the more used and longer length of rope, and this was best anyhow as it allowed for more slack for him to explore and had no knot that could wedge into gaps in the rock. The weather was still ideal, and the climbers still were in good condition as they climbed around the 10,500-foot mark. But the unexpected was about to take place. Carter later described what happened in those precious minutes before tragedy struck.

> Finally an apparent impasse was seen above by Dalgleish, and the writer unroped to give still more slack and freedom between Dalgleish and Brooks, who was tied in near the knot joining the two ropes. Lambert

also unroped and went up past Dalgleish to have a look at the situation. Dalgleish still roped to Brooks who with the writer was secured at the last belaying point some 50 feet below, then moved a few feet up to Lambert and they both decided that further progress in this direction was unjustified. The steepness of the buttress had necessitated careful climbing and it was now a few minutes before noon. The altitude was slightly over 10,500 ft. The party still felt quite fresh and the perfect weather and climbing conditions fully justified the carrying out of the proposed plan of retreating to the junction of a different route which had been chosen the previous day as an alternative. Lambert therefore descended, still unroped, to a small ledge immediately above where Brooks and the writer were waiting.

Dalgleish then commenced to descend, over the same route just taken by Lambert, while Brooks and the writer took in the slack rope over the belay. He had descended to within about 30 feet of the others when a slight scratching of nailed boots on the rocks above caused Lambert to look up just in time to see him disappear over the angle between the steep face of the buttress and its almost perpendicular side cliff that formed one wall of the snow gully that had been ascended earlier in the day. No exclamation or sound was heard as he fell. Brooks made a commendable effort to pull in the rope over the belay but did not succeed in gathering in more than a few feet when a terrific jerk which almost upset him occurred. He retained his grip on the rope, however, but the sliding of the taut rope down the sharp edge of a frost-shattered rock forming the angle of the buttress severed it within a few feet of his grasp. The rope, although it was the older of the two did not suddenly snap under the strain, and the parting took place some distance from both the belay and the knot joining the two ropes.[23]

The Alec Dalgleish memorial cairn at Icefall Point, 1935.

Much like the mountain had been unknown, and in many ways still was, so was the cause of Dalgleish's fall.

"Waddington had claimed its first victim," Chic Scott wrote. "The young man was buried in the snow, and a memorial cairn was erected at Icefall Point."[24]

CHAPTER 9:
WADDINGTON

There is nothing remarkable in the present-day appreciation of natural beauty, and in particular of mountain beauty. Man's love of Nature was certain to develop directly he began to emancipate himself from the grosser forms of materialism. It was not chance that directed his eyes to the hills; for thousands of years he had accepted Nature as something hostile and incalculable. Now he sees himself no longer as being on this planet by sufferance, but as a living part of a living universe. This knowledge enables him to draw spiritual consolation and comfort from all natural beauty.

—F.S. Smythe, *The Spirit of the Hills*

Neal Carter concluded his 1934 article about the fatal accident not by illustrating what knowledge had been gained about new routes or scientific discovery or the wonders of the natural world, as previous articles about expeditions to the mystery mountain had done. Instead, he voiced a concern about how the public was perceiving the character of the mountains. Simply put, he believed the public would now, as the result of the death of Dalgleish, perceive that the mountains were killing people. When this perception first took hold after the disaster on the descent of the Matterhorn in 1865, the golden age of Victorian mountaineering drew to an end. Would this disaster on Waddington spell the end for this active time for Canadian mountaineering, for these pilgrimages to Mount Waddington?

Carter had always relished exploration and was keen to advocate for the continued attempts at the final peak of Waddington. He took the opportunity, at the conclusion of his article, which many a mountaineer must have read as it covered a fatality on the peak that had captured the attention of climbers across North America and in the United Kingdom, to nip this perception problem in the bud.

In conclusion, a few words concerning the mountain may not be amiss. Three failures to ascend the still virgin peak during the summer of 1934 have left an unfortunate impression in the minds of those who have had to rely on the newspaper accounts of the attempts. The summit has been termed both "climbable" and "unclimbable." One face (the southeast) of this tower yet remains to be inspected at close range, and its accessibility from this general direction was considered quite feasible by the present party [Carter, Dalgleish, Lambert, Brooks] once the main ridge was gained. The day after the accident, it was shown by the party from Winnipeg (which was climbing the opposite face of the mountain quite unknown to the present party) that the base of the tower can be reached from the Interior approach. There is every evidence that one of the alternate routes to this face, approachable from the Pacific side, can be utilized.[1]

This tone of cooperation indicates a turning point, one where information might now be shared by expedition members, where the greater glory was not with the party but with the mountain. Chic Scott pointed out that "the Neave expedition had come the closest yet, and had opened the way for what, one day, would become the normal route up the mountain."[2] Carter continued his argument that the mountain, for which he had developed an affinity and respect, was best looked upon as an entity unto itself, and lest the mountaineering community get a bad name in public opinion, he left the last sentences to set the record straight. "The use of the adjective 'killer' as applied to Mt. Waddington both in the press and on the radio is no more appropriate than when applied to other mountains on which fatal accidents have occurred, e.g., Mt. Robson or the Matterhorn. The adjective 'unclimbable' as recently applied is certainly premature."[3]

This doubtful line of thinking about whether the final tower was unclimbable or not, combined with the public opinion surrounding the death of Dalgleish, a talented young man in his prime, was bolstered by an article by Don Munday in the same issue as Ferris Neave's article "New

Ways to Waddington" appeared. Simply titled "Mt. Waddington, 1934," Munday described his and Phyl's final foray into the Mount Waddington region, where a climb up the northwest peak (now dubbed the "Munday Summit") had him overlooking the final spire. The description given is chilling, and perhaps portrays a sealing of his conviction that, at least for the Mundays, the peak wasn't for them to climb first. It was a transition from optimism to pessimism. Whereas Don Munday's article about the 1933 expedition with Hall, "High Peaks of the Coast Range," had begun with the kind of optimism of which Carter would have approved ("Exploration is always exciting"[4]), "Mt. Waddington, 1934" had a darker tone to it.

Perhaps fitting for their final attempt on Mount Waddington, most of the Munday party would sail on the SS *Venture*, the Union steamship that had transported the Mundays up to Knight Inlet on their 1927 expedition. Joining them on the sail were their supporting porters for

Young "Pip" Brock and "Rod" Munro getting directions from Jim Stanton at Knight Inlet.

the expedition, Philip H.G. (Pip) Brock and Ronald R.N. (Rod) Munro; these young men were spry mountaineers in their own right. The Mundays were reunited at the Knight Inlet Cannery with Jim Stanton, who had been hospitable and helpful in the Mundays' earlier attempts on the peak. Pip and Rod eagerly lapped up what information Stanton had to offer, as he had "volunteered to take us 35 miles in his gas-boat to the mouth of the Franklin river where, on the 13th, we found landing much simplified by silting up of a formerly troublesome river channel."[5] Perhaps it was also fitting that Pip and Rod were with them, as they were indicative of a younger and more energetic generation of climbers who could decide whether Waddington was indeed "climbable" or not. Don Munday soon began referring to them in the article as the "boys." They proved very helpful in relaying gear up Franklin Glacier to a cache.

Meanwhile, Hall and Fuhrer were coming in by separate means, on another "gas-boat" operated by logger Jean Spiers, who had a logging

Franklin Glacier as viewed from the south side of Mount Waddington, 1935.

camp on the inlet. While the "boys" were relaying, Don and Phyl were in their rowboat, powered by an outboard motor, where they met with some trying times. Don wrote, "The engine failed us; we rowed against wind and tide until their increasing (and our decreasing) force defeated us at a rocky point. I tried to tow the boat past, perhaps having no happier time on wet limestone ledges hidden in seaweed than my wife did in her desperate fight to keep the boat from being smashed against the cliffs. Hall thought this an amusing variant of mountaineering when he sighted us, just before nightfall, from the gas-boat of Jean Spiers, a logger."[6]

The Carter/Dalgleish expedition had taken place but a few weeks prior. In fact, the death of Dalgleish had been indirectly responsible for the delay by a week of the Mundays' final expedition while "waiting to learn if our proffered help would be accepted in connection with giving more permanent burial to A.H. Dalgleish who had been killed on Mt. Waddington, June 26."[7] It would be hard to believe that this terrible event didn't inflict a pall on the Mundays' final attempt to climb Mt. Waddington.

With the Mundays' expedition team reunited at the glacier cache, they could begin in earnest. They unfortunately experienced rain and high winds. "We set out with first loads for a climbing camp on the 8th," Munday later wrote. "An hour's tramp up Franklin glacier took us to the base of Icefall point. We had rejected it as a site for base camp because of scanty fuel and exposed position in bad weather."[8]

Because the expeditions of the summer of 1934 were like the proverbial "ships that pass in the night" (from Henry Wadsworth Longfellow's poem "The Theologian's Tale"), the Mundays, Hall, and Fuhrer could not have benefitted from the knowledge gained in the expedition of just a few weeks previous. "At this time we did not know the Secord–Neave party had actually used the campsite we had considered at 10,500 feet on the ridge crest," Don Munday later wrote in the *Canadian Alpine Journal.* "The shortcoming of the southeast ridge consists in limiting attack solely to the always icy cliffs of the northeast face of the main (or central) peak."[9]

Historian Chic Scott noted that "by August 9 they were established at Little Alp Camp near the junction of the Dais and Franklin Glaciers." On August 10 the group, minus Pip and Ron, intended to climb the main peak. It was 4:10 a.m. when they set out, and already cloudy conditions

Mundays' climbing party approaching a daunting rock pinnacle near Mount Waddington, 1934.

and "cloud streamers" looked to be a bad omen to Don Munday, but so were the "huge ice-plumes" that could be seen on the summit towers. Nonetheless they moved forward. Chic Scott added that "they ascended the Dais Glacier to the bergschrund, then climbed the rocks of Waddington's southwest face to about 3500 metres [11,483 feet] before turning back."[10] The threat of being caught out, exposed on the slow-going rock of the icy final spire, despite the lack of new snow, went against Munday's climbing etiquette. "The rocks were free of snow; ledges incline too steeply for much to cling for long. The main couloir evidently leads up only into an alcove without indication of egress. Various patches of snow and ice hung in niches in the face above us but blank cliffs forbade linking them into a practicable route. At about 11,500 feet we turned back at 11:30 a.m. To be caught in bad weather on this face would be desperate; there are no belays and everything shelves outward steeply."[11]

On their descent, which had them breaking the snow's crust up to their thighs, they were pelted with ice fragments blown off the summit. Meeting Pip and Rod at camp, they found that the two had had a successful and productive day, making a first ascent of nearby Mount Cavalier.

At 3:20 a.m., with a clear canopy of stars above, the wind having blown the clouds away, the party got underway again. Don Munday fixed his gaze upon the final spire. "Over the central peak gleamed a lone star—I wondered if both were equally unattainable." Phyl and Don Munday were now committing to the route that they had taken in 1927–28. Phyl found a suspiciously familiar natural sculpture: In "the basin of 'Angel' glacier; Phyl once more discovered a sérac carven to seraphic semblance."[12]

Swinging their ice axes towards the northeast face of the final tower, Don's pessimism was growing based on experience and conditioning from their many sorties into the area beginning nearly a decade before. "Our knowledge of the mountain during eight seasons indicated, however, that the rocks were always very icy. We thought it well to see this peak from the northwest one."[13] After "a frontal attack on the steep face" brought the Mundays to a point where the ice seemed to take on qualities that captured the wonder they had seen in this region when exploring it for the first time, they admired "ice 'feathers' so fragile that blue light filtered up between one's feet." This delicate natural feature seemed to mirror Don Munday's failing strength of mind.

By 1:50 p.m. the Mundays achieved the same point on the northwest peak that they had reached in 1928, to some now known as the "Munday Summit." They stared directly at their nemesis, the final tower to the southeast. Don Munday seemed to regard it as something otherworldly now, a structure of unfathomable power, perhaps forbidden to all who might still have ambition to conquer this dagger of nature. He wrote a warning to other climbers.

> Only a few feet distant, the great spire poised in the void, an incredible nightmarish thing that must be seen to be believed, and then it is hard to believe; it is difficult to escape [the] appearance of exaggeration when dealing with a thing which in itself is an exaggeration. The mountain was in good condition—by Waddington's standard. Plates and plumes and festoons of ice

The south face of Mount Waddington from upper Dais Glacier, 1935.

"feathers" many feet thick draped even vertical rocks. In eight seasons we have never seen the summit free of its crumbling comb which may easily spell defeat when a climber is within less than a hundred feet of the final crest. Despite less favourable rock structure, the more ice-free southerly face may hold more hope than the ice-coated northerly wall. The southeasterly ridge of the tower is hopeless; the northwesterly one belies its distant appearance.[14]

To top off Munday's dispirited vision of his nemesis, smoke filled the background, the exhaust of some distant forest fire. The Mundays realized with resignation that they would not be the ones to summit the final spire of Waddington. But almost as a kind of redemption, Munday wrote that off in the distance, "perhaps nearly 70 miles away, we noted a range of nine or ten bold peaks ... I had not looked for such a thrill in revisiting the summit of Waddington."[15] There were other peaks to climb, just on the horizon. "For the present Mt. Waddington deserves to be rated as verging on the impossible when all factors are taken into account."[16]

In retrospect, Munday also believed that the climbing expedition of Ferris and Roger Neave, Campbell Secord, and Arthur Davidson deserved respect, even though while he was staring at the final peak he didn't know it had taken place. "At this time we did not know that the Secord–Neave party's splendid attempt confirmed our view of the severity of the climbing on the cliffs. One of the party told me their last 400 feet cost them nine hours; I understand they thought that they turned back 800 feet from the top: I judge it was nearer 600 feet, but I am convinced the remaining section would be still more difficult."[17]

Canadian mountaineering historian Chic Scott summed it up this way: "It was simply too difficult for them. The ascent would require all the paraphernalia and tricks of another generation."[18]

CHAPTER 10:

REALIZATIONS

The region within a fifty-mile radius of Mt. Waddington is today less peopled than even when Waddington began his trail. The heads of Bute and Knight inlets are visited in the fishing season by Indians from other reservations. The white population consists of three resident trappers, one being married. In Waddington's day Indians travelled back and forth through the Homathko Valley. Such travel has ceased and no continuous trail exists. The same applies to the central section of the Klinakline Valley to the west. For fifty years after the end of the Canadian Pacific Railway surveys there was no increase in important geographic knowledge of the region surrounding Mt. Waddington, and the written record was scanty in the extreme. The alpine areas remained unpenetrated until 1926 and 1927.

A great part of the heart of the Coast Range is entirely unsurveyed so far as alpine areas are concerned ... while the area known to mountaineers is a small fraction indeed: conditions below timberline all combine to discourage even climbers hardened to normal conditions of travel in the Range.[1]

—Don Munday, "Historical Sketch of Mt. Waddington Region"

On March 15, 1935, Phyl and Don Munday gave a lecture in Vancouver, partly about their final attempt on Mount Waddington the previous season, but also about what they had learned about their many forays in the region since 1925. The event was greatly anticipated, and members of the British Columbia Mountaineering Club were given the scoop on the front page of that year's March issue of *The B.C. Mountaineer*:

> An illustrated lecture on his latest trip to the Mount Waddington country will be given by Mr. Don Munday at the home of Mr. Phillip Brock, 3875 Point Grey Road, on Friday, March 15, at 8:30 p.m. Take the Fourth Avenue car to Alma Road, walk north to Point Grey Road two blocks (past Yacht Club). A series of exceptionally fine motion pictures and slides will be shown. As a courtesy to Mr. and Mrs. Brock those intending to be present are requested to add their names to the list which will be in the Club drawer at the Eastman Kodak Store.[2]

To this day, Brock House on Point Grey Road arranges for and presents illustrated author talks.

But this occasion marked an end of the Mundays' efforts that had made their name across Canada, North America, and the world of mountaineering. It was also a beginning of sorts, as they had encouraged and inspired a round of new expeditions to the area, perhaps partly for the glory of being the first on top of that final spire, but also in continuing the tradition, the pilgrimage begun ten years previous, of trying to attain that final peak.

The B.C. Mountaineer continued to cover the expeditions to the Waddington region. But unlike a decade before when editors such as Neal Carter were getting the initial stories of the celebrated mountaineer couple of their day into its pages, expeditions to the Mount Waddington region were now the fodder of articles beyond even the *Canadian Alpine Journal.* The *Sierra Club Bulletin*, published in San Francisco, was marking

Mount Waddington from Icefall Point, 1935.

expeditions in its bimonthly publication. In its February 1936 edition, "Mount Waddington," an article about a joint expedition with the British Columbia Mountaineering Club, got top billing, taking priority on page one over such glorious articles as "The Trinity Alps" and nudging ahead of an article featuring the words of an icon of American mountaineers in "Personal Recollections of John Muir." The Waddington story was even announced in the pages of *The Geographical Journal*, published in London, England, by the Royal Geographical Society in the form of a review of Sir Norman Watson's book *Round Mystery Mountain*, his account of the 1934 ski-mountaineering escapade up Scimitar Glacier that included Clifford White (pre-dating the Neave/Secord effort by just a few weeks). This review appeared in the September 1935 issue, with the November 1935 issue acknowledging the summer's overall attempts on the peak.

Not surprisingly then, the space taken up with accounts of the Waddington expeditions went beyond mere paragraphs in 1925 and 1926

Mount Waddington as seen from Dais Glacier, 1935.

to multi-issue feature stories within the pages of *The B.C. Mountaineer*. The pilgrimage to Mount Waddington was top-level stuff, and the number of resources being funnelled to fund the final spire's first ascent was growing.

Thus began the June 1936 issue of *The B.C. Mountaineer*, with Miss M. Jordan at the editorial helm: "For the first time in many years, the B.C. Mountaineering Club has definitely undertaken to sponsor an expedition directed at one of Canada's major mountain peaks." Inherent in Miss Jordan's front-page news was the understanding that the previous climbing season, the summer of 1935, the Sierra Club had given the peak a good college try. As mountaineering historian Chic Scott wrote, "In 1935 it was the turn of a group of climbers from the Sierra Club of California. Amongst the team were some of the best American climbers of the day: Bestor Robinson, David Brower, Jules Eichorn and Richard Leonard. After establishing a base camp on the Dais Glacier, they made two unsuccessful attempts on the south face, turned back the first time by a storm and the second time by poor conditions and falling ice. A third attempt via the Hall/Munday route reached the northwest summit but proceeded no further."[3]

The main peak's height was known in 1936 to be 13,260 feet, the northwest peak 13,200 feet. Although the name Mystery Mountain was still bandied about colloquially and locally, Mount Waddington was what it was known as internationally. Also known internationally was how many unsuccessful attempts had been made on the main peak. Jordan illustrated that while building up the anticipation of the 1936 joint expedition in the pages of *The B.C. Mountaineer*. "In the past ten years no fewer than thirteen parties have attempted to scale the 13,260 foot mountain," Jordan penned. What she was initiating, though, where previous buildup of expeditions had favoured simply reporting the who, what, and when of the plans, was reporting on the cooperation between growing numbers of men who all had been entranced by the efforts of Phyl and Don Munday, Sir Norman Watson and Clifford White, the Neave brothers and Campbell Secord, and others they would have read about. They wanted to participate in a tradition, a pilgrimage to a place where a kind of salvation was sought in the loveliness that had been written about by John Ruskin, John Muir, and pursued by legendary figures such as Edward Whymper. But despite their efforts, it was a place few could find solace. Jordan was acknowledging that it was only by working together, building on the previous struggles at Waddington, that success might be achieved. "Although unsuccessful," Jordan wrote, "they have all contributed to the increasing knowledge of possible routes and means of attack."[4]

The effort to generate this joint expedition of 1936 was considerable. Where previous efforts had been more informal affairs, this sortie had much previous organizational planning with both clubs. "For six months," wrote Jordan, "a hard-working committee has been planning the best method of approach, and final arrangements are nearing completion at the present time."

An advance party had already gone ahead by then with the priority of carrying food and gear in and setting up base camp, and the hope was that bolstered support would give climbers an improved chance. "Later

Sunrise over Franklin Glacier, facing Mount Sockeye (left) and Mount Agur (right), 1935.

in the month, the climbing party will follow in their footsteps and concentrate on the task of climbing the peak," wrote Jordan. "The inclusion in the party of several Sierra Club members should be a decided asset in tackling the final rock summit."[5]

The stakes seem to have been raised even more as a result of the publication of an article by Richard Leonard of the Sierra Club expedition of the previous summer, "Can Mt. Waddington be Climbed?" Never more explicitly had the question been posed and the implicit doubts placed in future climbers' minds. Within the article, Leonard acknowledged the cooperation that had taken place prior to the expedition through "correspondence with and advice from Henry S. Hall, Jr., Roger Neave, Eric Brooks, Don Munday and Colonel W.W. Foster."[6] His focus, though, seems to have been on the American contingent of the 1935 climb ("Seven climbers from the Sierra Club of California augmented by an eighth from the Harvard Mountaineering Club") and on describing, not

Mount Waddington viewed from Icefall Point, 1935.

Lawrence Grassi and Bill Dobson climb the south face of Mount Waddington, 1935.

A sunset at Icefall Point, Franklin Glacier, 1935.

unlike Don Munday had pointed out, how the final spire from the north-west summit had to be seen to be believed. "Their view of the terrifyingly steep pinnacle of rock and ice was tremendously impressive and convinced them that the summit would be an even more difficult climb than photographs had indicated."[7] However, Leonard concluded his article with a decidedly uplifting tone. "If an expert party of rock climbers with full piton equipment could ever find a day when the southwest face was free of ice they could climb rapidly to the final summit pitch."[8]

To meet the challenge, the 1936 joint expedition had an impressive lineup. Hervey Voge's article in the *Sierra Club Bulletin* provided the roll call. "The advance party comprised Jack Riegelhuth, Kenneth Adam, Hervey Voge, of the Sierra Club; William Taylor, of the B.C. Mountaineering Club, as botanist and cook; and Kenneth Austin, Denver Gillen, Donald Baker, of Vancouver, as packers. Baker went out when the second group came in. The second party comprised Bestor Robinson, Richard

M. Leonard, Raffi Bedayan, of the Sierra Club; William Dobson, James Irving, Elliot Henderson, of the B.C. Mountaineering Club; Lawrence Grassi, of the Alpine Club of Canada; and Arthur Mayse, a reporter, representing the 'Vancouver Province.'"[9]

Bill Dobson, in his own account in the August 1936 issue of *The B.C. Mountaineer*, offered a colourful announcement of the personnel of the joint expedition with a BCMC twist:

> On July 11th, the climbing party boarded the *Tranquilla* and departed from Vancouver, bearing with them the best wishes and hopes of the group of members and friends who had gathered on the wharf to see the boys away. The climbing party consisted of R.M. Leonard, R. Bedayan, and Bestor Robinson, of the Sierra Club, and J. Irving, E. Henderson, and W. Dobson of the B.C.M.C., with Lawrence Grassi, member of the Alpine Club of Canada, who had been invited to join the expedition. Robinson was in charge of the Sierra party, and Dobson in charge of the B.C. party. A previous arrangement of joint leadership had been agreed to by both Clubs. Somewhat unique in the annals of mountaineering was Arthur Mayse, news reporter for the *Vancouver Daily Province*, who also accompanied the expedition, complete with reams of writing paper and note books, to say nothing of carrier pigeons.[10]

However, there were rivals. In the 1936 *Canadian Alpine Journal*, vol. XXIV, Fritz H. Weissner wrote this introductory paragraph to his article: "In March 1936, several of my friends from the American Alpine Club asked me to join them and try the mountain the following summer. At the same time, unknown to us until some weeks later, another party, made up of some of the best climbers of the British Columbia Mountaineering Clubs [*sic*] and of the Sierra Club of California, the latter of which had made a fine attempt in 1935 were also organizing for an attack."[11] This climbing party, with the same intentions as the Dobson/Robinson party, was very close by. "A veritable flower garden flourished at Icefall Point. Among the blossoms we established the base camp, and made

The climbing party boarded the *Tranquilla*, departing Vancouver, July 11, 1936.

ready to attack the nearby peaks," Hervey Voge remarked. "Beside us, in friendly proximity, were camped members of a rival climbing party: Fritz Weissner, William House, Elizabeth Woolsey, and Alanson Wilcox. They also had Mount Waddington as their goal, yet as a matter of courtesy they granted us the first chance at the mountain. Our friendly relations with them, typified by many tea parties and long discussions, constituted one of the great pleasures of the trip. Would that all competition could be characterized by such fellowship."[12]

"After some friendly correspondence both parties agreed that they should go through with their plans," wrote Fritz Weissner, "and as the other party included climbers who had tried the mountain before, we agreed that they should have the first chance."[13]

The B.C. Mountaineer characterized the expedition as hopeful, but it tempered that with the disappointments of the past. "If it is humanly possible to conquer the hitherto impregnable summit, and given a break

An unidentified climber in front of the main tower of Mount Waddington from the slopes of Snow Peak, 1935.

by the weather, they will do it," wrote M. Jordan.[14] The publication stretched out the account of the expedition into several installments, keeping the readers of the BCMC membership glued to their newsletters from August 1936 to January 1937, beginning with Bill Dobson's introduction to his August 1936 article "Mount Waddington Expedition":

> Eyes of mountaineers throughout the world have centred for the past 10 years on the great peaks of B.C.'s Coast Range; particularly on Mount Waddington, whose slender summit rises almost 500 feet above its nearest rival. Evidence of interest shown in the hitherto virgin summit can be found in articles in numerous outstanding European mountaineering publications. Twelve repulsed attempts and uncertainty in the minds of many experienced climbers as to the possibility of reaching the summit, have only served as an incentive to fire the ambitions of climbers near and far.
>
> Situated only a few hundred miles north of Vancouver, it was felt by many that the time had come when the B.C.M.C. should take some interest in this great peak so close at hand. Late in 1935 plans began to materialize for an attack on the mountain during the summer of 1936.[15]

The Sierra Club climbing party with Bestor Robinson leading and the British Columbia climbing party with Bill Dobson leading went their own ways. "The parties wished each other success and parted, after agreeing to go as far as possible and reconnoitre but deciding to return before darkness enforced a bivouac on the rocks," Dobson later wrote. "A night on the face of Waddington would be not only unpleasant, but serious in the event of storm, and quite unjustified if at all preventable."[16]

While those parties sought their fortunes, the Weissner/House party made the best of the day by making a new camp. "We used the day to carry supplies up over the upper, steeper and crevassed part of Dais Glacier," recalled Fritz Weissner, "and established a one tent camp approximately 400 feet below the bergschrund."[17] There they decided their group would try the mountain in pairs, with Weissner and House making up the first

The loose, rocky terrain of the south face of Mount Waddington.

reconnoitring climb. The American Alpine Club party watched as members of Dobson's British Columbia party and the Sierra Club party struggled. The latter two "parties were doomed to failure and disappointment" was the final verdict.[18] They returned just before the light of day faded. July 20 saw Weissner and House leaving their camp below the bergschrund at 3:30 a.m. for their attempt. They braved the climb up rotten and ice-glazed rock, but ultimately had to return to their camp.

On July 21, they struck lower Dais Glacier camp and another camp at 10,800 feet was established by Dobson's party. With a hard snow crust, they hoped for efficient and productive climbing. But on this day they had to watch the Weissner/House party, who left camp at 2:45 a.m. and crossed the bergschrund by 3:30 a.m., do what no one had been able to do up to that point: reach the summit. Dobson acknowledged the historic value of the Weissner/House party's achievement. How could he not?

> This was an eventful day in the annal of North American mountaineering, for on this day, Fritz H. Wiessner and William P. House gained the summit of B.C.'s foremost peak. At 10 a.m. in the morning we observed them with the glasses, high on the mountain, forging slowly but surely towards their goal. Their route was hard and difficult and at 2 p.m., four hours later, they appeared to have gained little more than two or three hundred feet. The sound of numerous loosened rocks, crashing down the cliffs, told us much about the difficulties they were encountering and also made us wonder about the statements of some previous parties, that scarcely a loose rock could be found on Waddington's south face. We had been troubled with loose rock on our first acquaintance with the mountain several days before ...
>
> At dusk of the evening before, Wiessner and House were observed on the mountain coming down, but at such an altitude that it seemed frankly certain that they would be forced to bivouac. As it happened, the night was fairly light and enabled them to perform the almost

Mount Waddington from the lower Dais Glacier camp during the British Columbia Mountaineering Club party's attempt on the peak, 1935.

impossible feat of descending and roping down in the dark. We were unaware that they had come down, and whereas we had planned to use the same couloir that Wiessner used, we now altered our plans as we had no intention of offering ourselves as targets for stones from a party supposedly above us. Wiessner and House arrived in camp shortly before we arose; we probably missed them by a scant half hour.[19]

The climb by Weissner and House was not without its own struggle, but certainly experience and state-of-the-art climbing technology, including Eckenstein crampons, were to their advantage. Without question, the reconnaissance of previous climbing parties over the past decade had supported these two expert climbers. Chic Scott backs up that view in his history of Canadian mountaineering: "But the truth remained that for most of these parties the extreme nature of the climbing had put the summit beyond their reach, and it was really the skill and technique of Fritz Wiessner, learned and perfected in the crucible of the European Alps, that led to success."[20]

———————•———————

Phyllis and Don Munday's lecture event at the home of Mr. and Mrs. Brock on Point Grey Road in Vancouver on March 15, 1935, was a rousing success. "A large number of club members and friends attended the illustrated lecture given by Mr. and Mrs. Munday," editor J.N. Betts wrote in *The B.C. Mountaineer*. What was perhaps most remarkable was the photographic record on display, images captured by the Mundays. At this time Phyl was still the honorary photographic secretary for the Alpine Club of Canada. "Mrs. Munday gave us a vivid and interesting description of the most recent expedition to the Mount Waddington area. The story was illustrated by a beautiful series of slides shown by Mr. Munday. Among the more striking pictures were the close-ups of the ice plastered summit tower taken from the northwest peak."[21]

AFTERWORD

As they watched, the dying Sun-God
Sank below a distant col,
Projecting demons on the snowfields,
Leaking forth in cosmic pall
To bathe the ageless icefields
In its bleary red flood,
To gild the gruesome gargoyles
With the sickening hue of blood

—Dick Culbert, "From Something Other, to Something Sought"[1]

T hinkers during the Victorian era such as John Ruskin were highly influential in persuading their readers that nature was not something otherworldly, a place devoid of spirituality, but a place where, perhaps, spirituality already existed. In North America, John Muir, a mountaineer, naturalist, and writer of renown, was very convincing in his argument that humanity must preserve nature. Perhaps more important and influential was his belief that nature was not a godless place, but a place where the sacred could be found.

There is something to be said about how the immense natural spaces of the Pacific slope of North America, specifically its mountainous regions, alter a spirituality that may have come from something more institutional, making it more inclusive and accessible, at least for those courageous and adventurous enough to seek it. Don and Phyllis Munday embodied this heroism in their initial attempts on Mystery Mountain—later Mount Waddington—and captured the public's spirit. It was a public emerging from the Victorian era and the First World War, and people were in search of something new. The mountaineering couple represented seeking something new yet elusive, something that many of the public were seeking themselves. The recent creation of mountaineering clubs, the founding of the Alpine Club of Canada in 1906 and the British Columbia Mountaineering Club in 1907, indicated an awakening in this regard. Figures such as the Mundays were followed by the Neave brothers, who made a pilgrimage from the very foundations of the Alpine Club of Canada in Winnipeg to seek out the daunting and forbidding image of the final spire.

Indigenous Peoples on the west coast of North America, who have lived there since time immemorial, have known this spirituality since long before the arrival of Europeans. A harmony with nature and an understanding of the spiritual value of nature had been established well before mountaineers became interested in attaining the highest of the high peaks in North America. As historian Jean Barman has written, the means for doing this were twofold through "their relationship to the land and their spirituality."[2] Could mountaineers, their descendants, and recent arrivals from distant shores have also been seeking a deity, something to follow in this land that, at least to them, was new and, in its vastness, unknown and forbidding? The very name of Mystery Mountain expresses that: an excitement for what was out there that permeated explorers' hearts and minds for much of the twentieth century. As Austrian-born legendary mountain guide Conrad Kain once said, "I find my God in the stillness of nature." There was something up there that was elusive, impalpable, ineffable.

On the subject of glaciers in the Yosemite region in California, John Muir's writing is full of descriptions of the pristine and the sublime, as well as the accomplishments and benefits of healthy exercise and the "clear, death-like sleep of the tired mountaineer." He also often compares the geologic and related constructions of the natural world to cathedrals and other human-made places of worship, alluding to their worthiness as places to explore, places to which a man could make a pilgrimage. How could the armchair traveller or the potential adventurer or mountaineer in the 1890s not be persuaded by the descriptions of his explorations of the mountain glaciers of the Yosemite?

> Early next morning I set out to trace the grand old glacier
> that had done so much for the beauty of the Yosemite
> region back to its farthest fountains, enjoying the charm

that every explorer feels in Nature's untrodden wilder-
nesses. The voices of the mountains were still asleep.
The wind scarce stirred the pine-needles. The sun was
up, but it was yet too cold for the birds and the few
burrowing animals that dwell here. Only the stream,
cascading from pool to pool, seemed to be wholly awake.
Yet the spirit of the opening day called to action. The
sunbeams came streaming gloriously through the jagged
openings of the col, glancing on the burnished pave-
ments and lighting the silvery lakes, while every sun-
touched rock burned white on its edges like melting
iron in a furnace.[3]

Also note his personification of the mountains themselves, or perhaps
more accurately his allusion to their consciousness as deities or mythological figures who sleep and may be awoken, perhaps even displeased.
Although crevasses were looked on with dread by mountaineers of the
age of the Mundays and the Neaves for the inevitable delays or dangers
they represented, Muir was enthralled with them and made them out to
be subterranean paths to a mythological realm.

A series of rugged zigzags enabled me to make my way
down into the weird under-world of the crevasse. Its
chambered hollows were hung with a multitude of
clustered icicles, amid which pale, subdued light pulsed
and shimmered with indescribable loveliness. Water
dripped and tinkled overhead, and from far below came
strange, solemn murmurings from currents that were
feeling their way through veins and fissures in the dark.
The chambers of a glacier are perfectly enchanting, not-
withstanding one feels out of place in their frosty beauty.[4]

To a mainly Christian, churchgoing readership, this comparison
must have been influential, pointing out the similarities to a sacred place
rather than to the savageries of the natural world. It was a place where
the average person, with an adventurous soul and a purity of heart, could
find their footing, both physically and spiritually. One need not fear the

snow either. Muir calls upon the mountaineer-to-be with a description
of snow conditions at the end of spring that allows for accessibility to
what may have been seen in the recent past as forbidding.

> At the end of June only here and there may the moun-
> taineer find a secure snow-bridge. The most lasting of
> the winter bridges, thawing from below as well as from
> above, because of warm currents of air passing through
> the tunnels, are strikingly arched and sculptured; and
> by the occasional freezing of the oozing, dripping water
> of the ceiling they become brightly and picturesquely
> icy. In some of the reaches, where there is a free margin,
> we may walk through them. Small skylights appearing
> here and there, these tunnels are not very dark. The
> roaring river fills all the arching way with impressively
> loud reverberating music, which is sweetened at times
> by the ouzel, a bird that is not afraid to go wherever a
> stream may go, and to sing wherever a stream sings.[5]

Here is not only found familiar beauty, as one might find in a regular
place of worship in an urban centre, but a sense of transformation of
that which is considered savage and unstable to something aesthetically
and sensorially pleasing. Instead of an organ, there is the river. Instead
of a choir, there is a lively bird.

But perhaps the pièce de résistance is to be found in John Muir's
descriptions of the heights in "My First Summer in the Sierra." Here
the reader is transported to a place where there are no troubles and
where one can find, in more mindful moments, deliverance, absolution,
and a kind of forgiveness.

> No pain here, no dull empty hours, no fear of the past,
> no fear of the future. These blessed mountains are so
> compactly filled with God's beauty, no petty personal
> hope or experience has room to be. Drinking this cham-
> pagne water is pure pleasure, so is breathing the living
> air, and every movement of limbs is pleasure, while the
> whole body seems to feel beauty when exposed to it as

it feels the campfire or sunshine, entering not by the eyes alone, but equally through all one's flesh like radiant heat, making a passionate, ecstatic pleasure-glow not explainable. One's body then seems homogenous throughout, sound as a crystal.[6]

The imagery here, and Muir's conveying of the grandeur of the mountains, was wont to set a sleepy populace, bound to an industrial future, afire with dreams of wide-open spaces such as Yosemite, and also to yearn and search for those that had yet to be trodden. Where else might these places of solace exist? Should it not be the pursuit of the urban adventurer to regain a part of themselves there? Are these the places where, collectively, we can become whole again?

Could the Mundays have caught on to this movement? It was a movement that had begun with the thinkers and adventurers in Europe and made its way over to North America. There, it developed into a kind of preservatory whirlwind that was solidified and became a spiritual movement through the arrival of newcomers to a place of vast natural beauty, where the remnants of institutional religion from the Old World were being transformed into something new. Could this have promulgated the pilgrimage in a 1930 Plymouth of the Neave brothers, Cam Secord, and Arthur Davidson, who were not, collectively at least, the most experienced of mountaineers? In none of my research have I read of any of these climbers mentioning churchgoing. This is not to say they did not attend traditional spiritual centres, but my conclusion is that their place of worship was to be found elsewhere, in those untrodden places where spirituality already exists. Finally, it was a movement trying to find familiarity in older, European imagery; for example, finding familiarity in the Waddington region by referring to it as "Matterhorn-like."

It has been said that Canada did not have the equivalent of a preservationist and spiritual thinker like the American John Muir. Perhaps Canada's closest equivalents were Phyl and Don Munday through their writing, photographs, and deeds, and through their leadership by example. As British Columbia author and mountaineer Ron Dart points out in his book *Mountaineering and the Humanities*, Don Munday didn't only write about geology or the mechanics of mountaineering in a linear fashion, he pointed out the spiritual in the mountains. "Don's article[s] in such periodicals as *British Columbia Digest, The British Ski Year Book* and *The Geographical Review* highlight the fact that Don never severed the actual climb from observations on the climb or from personal and literary reflections about the meaning of the peaks."[7]

Yet it's likely the meaning behind the mountains might not have become so idealized without the English Romantics of the Victorian era. John Ruskin was a writer who thought on a wide variety of subjects, and even though his ambitions did not take him into the high altitudes that motivated his contemporaries like Edward Whymper, he was an influential figure in presenting the high peaks as a place where spirituality could be sought. As Ron Dart points out, "Ruskin, like the High Romantics, blended the well-told tales of nature, the rocky crags and a wise notion of the economy. *Modern Painters*, by Ruskin, has two challenging chapters (Book V: chapters 19–20) on the shift from a Classical tradition that seemed to ignore Nature to the Romantic tradition that turned to Nature as a sacred place of glory and all that is good."[8]

Ruskin, who had a sharp awareness of nature attuned to its value, followed up his writing in *Modern Painters* with a body of work on the subject of politics. Combined, his writing encapsulated a time and was part of a movement that brought the political, the social, the economic, and the natural together in ways that are still relevant today. "Ruskin's political writings were basic building blocks for the foundation of the Labour Party in England," wrote Dart. "It is essential, therefore, that we connect the thoughts, lives and writings of the English High Romantics and Ruskin. Their integrated vision of nature, land, peaks and politics cannot be missed or ignored. They prepared the way for the ecological and environmental movements of our day and a broader vision of politics that calls the state to be involved in bringing about the common good."[9]

Whether the quartet of Winnipeg climbers who piled into that 1930 Plymouth in 1934 had the common good in mind when they set out for Tatlayoko Lake is anybody's guess, but what they did have was an inner spirit. This spirit may have also been what made Winnipeg, distant from the Rockies, the Purcells, and the Coast Mountains of British Columbia, the foundational centre for mountaineering in Canada. A yearning, a craving for what lay beyond the horizon and the journey to get there, was inherent in organizations like the Alpine Club of Canada and, regionally, the British Columbia Mountaineering Club. These were assemblies of groups comprising individuals who longed to connect with nature, not necessarily for their own glory, but to glorify and accentuate nature, and to further know themselves.

NOTES

Acknowledgements

1. "Homalco History: Read about the history of the Homalco People," Homalco First Nation, accessed October 25, 2024, https://www.homalco.com/who-we-are/history/.
2. P. Munday, "Old Ways to Waddington."

Introduction

1. Clark, *Victorian Mountaineers*, 61.
2. Clark, *Victorian Mountaineers*, 18.
3. Clark, *Victorian Mountaineers*, 36.
4. Clark, *Victorian Mountaineers*, 73.
5. Clark, *Victorian Mountaineers*, 20.
6. Clark, *Victorian Mountaineers*, 21.
7. Clark, *Victorian Mountaineers*, 21–22.
8. Ruskin, *Modern Painters*, 422.
9. Clark, *Victorian Mountaineers*, 40.
10. Clark, *Victorian Mountaineers*, 113.
11. Clark, *Victorian Mountaineers*, 73.
12. Clark, *Victorian Mountaineers*, 123.
13. Clark, *Victorian Mountaineers*, 124.
14. Clark, *Victorian Mountaineers*, 127.
15. Clark, *Victorian Mountaineers*, 128.
16. Clark, *Victorian Mountaineers*, 129.

17. Clark, *Victorian Mountaineers*, 131.

18. Clark, *Victorian Mountaineers*, 138.

19. Smythe, *Edward Whymper*, 1–3.

20. Johnson, *Not-So-Savage Land*, 1.

21. Johnson, *Not-So-Savage Land*, 32–33.

22. Johnson, *Not-So-Savage Land*, 43.

23. Johnson, *Not-So-Savage Land*, 45.

24. Johnson, *Not-So-Savage Land*, 45.

25. F. Whymper, *Travel and Adventure in the Territory of Alaska*, viii.

26. F. Whymper, *Travel and Adventure in the Territory of Alaska*, 18.

27. F. Whymper, *Travel and Adverture in the Territory of Alaska*, 18.

28. A. Scott, *The Encyclopedia of Raincoast Place Names*, 267–68.

29. F. Whymper, *Travel and Adventure in the Territory of Alaska*, 19.

30. F. Whymper, *Travel and Adventure in the Territory of Alaska*, 21.

31. F. Whymper, *Travel and Adventure in the Territory of Alaska*, 24.

32. F. Whymper, *Travel and Adventure in the Territory of Alaska*, 26–27.

Chapter 1

1. D. Munday, *Unknown Mountain*, 4.

2. D. Munday, "Mt. Arrowsmith," 3.

3. D. Munday, "Mt. Arrowsmith," 3.

4. D. Munday, "Mt. Arrowsmith," 3.

5. D. Munday, "Mt. Arrowsmith," 3.

6. D. Munday, "Mt. Arrowsmith," 3.

7. D. Munday, "Exploration in the Coast Range," 121.

8. D. Munday, "Exploration in the Coast Range," 121.

9. D. Munday, "Exploration in the Coast Range," 121–22.

10. Foster, "Invading the Mountains of Bute Inlet," 4.

11. Foster, "Invading the Mountains of Bute Inlet," 4.

12. Foster, "Invading the Mountains of Bute Inlet," 4.

13. P. Munday, "Old Ways to Waddington."

14. D. Munday, *Unknown Mountain*, 4.

15. Henry, *Good Company*, 43–46.

16. D. Munday, *Unknown Mountain*, 6.

17. D. Munday, *Unknown Mountain*, 6.

18. D. Munday, *Unknown Mountain*, 7.

19. D. Munday, *Unknown Mountain*, 11.

20. P. Munday, "Old Ways to Waddington."

21. P. Munday, "Old Ways to Waddington."

22. D. Munday, *Unknown Mountain*, 8.

23. P. Munday, "First Ascent of Mt. Robson by Lady Members," 68.

24. Bridge, *Passion for Mountains*, 128–29.

25. P. Munday, "First Ascent of Mt. Robson by Lady Members," 68.

26. P. Munday, "First Ascent of Mt. Robson by Lady Members," 68.

27. P. Munday, "First Ascent of Mt. Robson by Lady Members," 72.

28. Carter, "Still a Mystery," 4.

29. D. Munday, *Unknown Mountain*, 17.

30. D. Munday, *Unknown Mountain*, 11.

31. D. Munday, *Unknown Mountain*, 17.

32. D. Munday, *Unknown Mountain*, 17–18.

33. D. Munday, *Unknown Mountain*, 20.

34. In fact, August Schnarr's three daughters raised two cougars as pets, part of a litter of four of which two had died. Williams, *Cougar Companions*.

35. D. Munday, *Unknown Mountain*, 22.

36. D. Munday, *Unknown Mountain*, 22.

37. Carter, "An Expedition," 4.

38. Bridge, *Passion for Mountains*, 164.

39. D. Munday, "Exploration in the Coast Range," 4.

40. D. Munday, "Exploration in the Coast Range," 4.

41. P. Munday, "Old Ways to Waddington."

42. D. Munday, "Exploration in the Coast Range," 4.

43. P. Munday, "Old Ways to Waddington."

44. D. Munday, "Exploration in the Coast Range," 4.

45. D. Munday, "Exploration in the Coast Range," 4.

46. D. Munday, "Exploration in the Coast Range," 4.

47 Huggard, "Lecture on Mystery Mountain," 2.

48. D. Munday, "Mystery Mountain," 1.

49. D. Munday, "Mystery Mountain," 1.

50. Wheeler, "Rogers Pass at the Summit of the Selkirks," 48.

51. Woods, "Sierra Climbers on Waddington," 23.

52. D. Munday, "Mystery Mountain," 1.

Chapter 2

1. Twain, *A Tramp Abroad*, 222–23.
2. Taylor, "Accident on Little Goat," 2.
3. Taylor, "Accident on Little Goat," 2.
4. D. Munday, *Unknown Mountain*, 78.
5. D. Munday, *Unknown Mountain*, 78.
6. D. Munday, "The Apex of the Coast Range," 1.
7. P. Munday, "Old Ways to Waddington."
8. D. Munday, "The Apex of the Coast Range," 1.
9. D. Munday, *Unknown Mountain*, 80.
10. D. Munday, "The Apex of the Coast Range," 2.
11. D. Munday, "The Apex of the Coast Range," 1.
12. D. Munday, "The Apex of the Coast Range," 1.
13. D. Munday, "The Apex of the Coast Range," 2.
14. D. Munday, "The Apex of the Coast Range," 3.
15. D. Munday, "The Apex of the Coast Range," 4.
16. D. Munday, *Unknown Mountain*, 85.
17. D. Munday, "The Apex of the Coast Range," 5.
18. D. Munday, "The Apex of the Coast Range," 5.
19. D. Munday, *Unknown Mountain*, 97–98.
20. D. Munday, *Unknown Mountain*, 97–98.
21. D. Munday, *Unknown Mountain*, 94.
22. D. Munday, *Unknown Mountain*, 94.
23. D. Munday, *Unknown Mountain*, 94–95.
24. D. Munday, *Unknown Mountain*, 92.
25. D. Munday, *Unknown Mountain*, 92.
26. Betts, "Red-Snow and Ice-Worms," 4.
27. Betts, "Red-Snow and Ice-Worms," 4.
28. Betts, "Red-Snow and Ice-Worms," 4.
29. D. Munday, "The Apex of the Coast Range," 7–8.
30. D. Munday, "The Apex of the Coast Range," 8.
31. D. Munday, "The Apex of the Coast Range," 8.
32. D. Munday, "The Apex of the Coast Range," 8.
33. D. Munday, "The Apex of the Coast Range," 9.
34. D. Munday, "The Apex of the Coast Range," 9–10.
35. D. Munday, "The Apex of the Coast Range," 11.

36. D. Munday, "The Apex of the Coast Range," 11.
37. Skelton, "Archival Highlights: Malcolm Geddes."
38. D. Munday, "The Apex of the Coast Range," 15.

Chapter 3

1. Spouse, "Mt. Waddington Conquered," 3.
2. D. Munday, "Heart of the Coast Range," 3.
3. D. Munday, "Heart of the Coast Range," 3.
4. D. Munday, "Heart of the Coast Range," 3.
5. Scott, *Pushing the Limits*, 111.
6. D. Munday, "Heart of the Coast Range," 4.
7. Bridge, *Passion for Mountains*, 178.
8. Scott, *Pushing the Limits*, 111.
9. Bridge, *Passion for Mountains*, 180.
10. D. Munday, "Mt. Waddington," 9.
11. Bridge, *Passion for Mountains*, 180.
12. Cooper, "The Relation of Skiing to Mountaineering," 1.
13. D. Munday, "Ski-Climbs in the Coast Range," 101.
14. Bridge, *Passion for Mountains*, 182.
15. D. Munday, "Ski-Climbs in the Coast Range," 111.
16. D. Munday, *Unknown Mountain*, 191.
17. D. Munday, "High Peaks of the Coast Range," 1.
18. Hall, "1934 Attempts on Mount Waddington," 298.
19. Scott, *Pushing the Limits*, 112.
20. D. Munday, "High Peaks of the Coast Range," 13.
21. D. Munday, "High Peaks of the Coast Range," 14–15.
22. Hall, "1934 Attempts on Mount Waddington," 299–300.

Chapter 4

1. F. Neave, "New Ways to Waddington," 32.
2. F. Neave, *Waddington Expedition Diary*, May 27, 1934, entry.
3. R. Neave, interview.
4. F. Neave, "New Ways to Waddington," 32.
5. R. Neave, interview.
6. F. Neave, *Waddington Expedition Diary*, May 27, 1934, entry.
7. R. Neave, interview.

8. R. Neave, interview.

9. Scott, *Pushing the Limits*, 66–67.

10. R. Neave, interview.

11. Parker, *"Roger Neave: Pioneer Mountaineer,"* 42.

12. Parker, *"Roger Neave: Pioneer Mountaineer,"* 43.

13. F. Neave, *Waddington Expedition Diary*, May 27, 1934, entry.

14. F. Neave, *Waddington Expedition Diary*, May 28, 1934, entry.

15. F. Neave, "Spring Snows of the Yoho," 122.

16. F. Neave, "Spring Snows of the Yoho," 123.

17. F. Neave, *Waddington Expedition Diary*, May 28, 1934, entry.

18. F. Neave, *Waddington Expedition Diary*, May 28, 1934, entry.

19. F. Neave, *Waddington Expedition Diary*, May 28, 1934, entry.

20. Watson and King, *Round Mystery Mountain*, 37.

21. Watson and King, *Round Mystery Mountain*, 37.

22. F. Neave, *Waddington Expedition Diary*, May 29, 1934, entry.

23. Betts, "Mount Seymour Trip," 2.

24. Betts, "Attempt on Mt. Waddington," 3.

25. Carter, "Fatal Accident on Mt. Waddington," 46.

26. F. Neave, "New Ways to Waddington," 32.

27. F. Neave, "In Memoriam: Alexander Addison McCoubrey," 81.

28. McCoubrey, "Purcell Pilgrimage," 74.

29. Ricker, "Dr. Ferris Neave, F.R.S.C.," 56.

30. Ricker, "Dr. Ferris Neave, F.R.S.C.," 58.

31. F. Neave, *Waddington Expedition Diary*, May 29, 1934, entry.

32. R. Neave, interview.

33. F. Neave, *Waddington Expedition Diary*, May 30, 1934, entry.

34. F. Neave, *Waddington Expedition Diary*, May 30, 1934, entry.

35. F. Neave, "New Ways to Waddington," 32.

36. F. Neave, "In Memoriam," 52.

37. McCoubrey, "Purcell Pilgrimage," 19.

38. F. Neave, *Waddington Expedition Diary*, May 30, 1934, entry.

39. F. Neave, *Waddington Expedition Diary*, June 1, 1934, entry.

Chapter 5

1. Smythe, *Spirit of the Hills*, 12.

2. F. Neave, *Waddington Expedition Diary*, June 1, 1934, entry.

3. F. Neave, *Waddington Expedition Diary*, June 1, 1934, entry.

4. R. Neave, interview.

5. Scott, *Pushing the Limits*, 113.

6. F. Neave, "New Ways to Waddington," 32–33.

7. F. Neave, "New Ways to Waddington," 33.

8. F. Neave, "New Ways to Waddington," 33.

9. F. Neave, *Waddington Expedition Diary*, June 3, 1934, entry.

10. F. Neave, *Waddington Expedition Diary*, June 3, 1934, entry.

11. R. Neave, interview.

12. F. Neave, *Waddington Expedition Diary*, June 3, 1934, entry.

13. F. Neave, *Waddington Expedition Diary*, June 3, 1934, entry.

14. F. Neave, "New Ways to Waddington," 33.

15. F. Neave, *Waddington Expedition Diary*, June 4, 1934, entry.

16. R. Neave, interview.

17. F. Neave, *Waddington Expedition Diary*, June 5, 1934, entry.

18. F. Neave, *Waddington Expedition Diary*, June 5, 1934, entry.

19. Leslie, *In the Western Mountains*, 62.

20. F. Neave, *Waddington Expedition Diary*, June 5, 1934, entry.

21. F. Neave, *Waddington Expedition Diary*, June 6, 1934, entry.

22. Leslie, *In the Western Mountains*, 63.

23. F. Neave, *Waddington Expedition Diary*, June 6, 1934, entry.

24. F. Neave, "New Ways to Waddington," 34.

25. F. Neave, *Waddington Expedition Diary*, June 6, 1934, entry.

26. D. Munday, *Unknown Mountain*, 22.

27. Williams, *Cougar Companions*, 48.

28. Williams, *Cougar Companions*, 2.

29. R. Neave, interview.

30. F. Neave, *Waddington Expedition Diary*, June 6, 1934, entry.

31. F. Neave, *Waddington Expedition Diary*, June 7, 1934, entry.

32. R. Neave, interview.

33. F. Neave, "New Ways to Waddington," 34.

34. F. Neave, "New Ways to Waddington," 34.

35. F. Neave, *Waddington Expedition Diary*, June 8, 1934, entry.

36. F. Neave, *Waddington Expedition Diary*, June 8, 1934, entry.

37. F. Neave, *Waddington Expedition Diary*, June 9, 1934, entry.

38. F. Neave, *Waddington Expedition Diary*, June 10, 1934, entry.

39. F. Neave, "New Ways to Waddington," 34.

40. F. Neave, *Waddington Expedition Diary*, June 11, 1934, entry.

41. F. Neave, *Waddington Expedition Diary*, June 12, 1934, entry.

42. F. Neave, "New Ways to Waddington," 35.

43. F. Neave, *Waddington Expedition Diary*, June 13, 1934, entry.

44. F. Neave, *Waddington Expedition Diary*, June 13, 1934, entry.

45. F. Neave, "New Ways to Waddington," 35

46. F. Neave, "New Ways to Waddington," 35

47. F. Neave, "New Ways to Waddington," 36.

48. F. Neave, *Waddington Expedition Diary*, June 15, 1934, entry.

49. F. Neave, *Waddington Expedition Diary*, June 15, 1934, entry.

50. F. Neave, *Waddington Expedition Diary*, June 17, 1934, entry.

51. F. Neave, "New Ways to Waddington," 36.

52. F. Neave, "New Ways to Waddington," 36.

53. F. Neave, "New Ways to Waddington," 36.

54. F. Neave, "New Ways to Waddington," 32.

55. F. Neave, "New Ways to Waddington," 37.

56. F. Neave, *Waddington Expedition Diary*, June 18, 1934, entry.

57. F. Neave, *Waddington Expedition Diary*, June 18, 1934, entry.

58. F. Neave, "New Ways to Waddington," 37.

59. F. Neave, *Waddington Expedition Diary*, June 18, 1934, entry.

60. F. Neave, "New Ways to Waddington," 37.

61. F. Neave, "New Ways to Waddington," 37.

Chapter 6

1. Smythe, *Spirit of the Hills*, 207.

2. Hall, "Coast Range," 97.

3. Hall, "Coast Range," 105.

4. E. Whymper, *Scrambles Amongst the Alps*, 318.

5. F. Neave, *Waddington Expedition Diary*, June 20, 1934, entry.

6. F. Neave, "New Ways to Waddington," 37.

7. F. Neave, *Waddington Expedition Diary*, June 20, 1934, entry.

8. F. Neave, "New Ways to Waddington," 38.

9. R. Neave, interview.

10. F. Neave, *Waddington Expedition Diary*, June 21, 1934, entry.

11. F. Neave, "New Ways to Waddington," 38.

12. Forde, "Hints on the Use of the Rope," June 1927, 4.

13. R. Neave, interview.

14. R. Neave, interview.

15. R. Neave, interview.

16. R. Neave, interview.

17. R. Neave, interview.

18. F. Neave, *Waddington Expedition Diary*, June 24, 1934, entry.

19. F. Neave, "New Ways to Waddington," 38.

20. R. Neave, interview.

21. F. Neave, "New Ways to Waddington," 39.

22. F. Neave, "New Ways to Waddington," 39.

23. R. Neave, interview.

24. Forde, "Hints on the Use of the Rope," March 1927, 4.

25. Forde, "Hints on the Use of the Rope," May 1927, 3.

26. F. Neave, "New Ways to Waddington," 39.

Chapter 7

1. Smythe, *Spirit of the Hills*, 129.

2. Forde, "Hints on the Use of the Rope," May 1927, 4.

3. F. Neave, "New Ways to Waddington," 40.

4. R. Neave, interview.

5. F. Neave, *Waddington Expedition Diary*, June 26, 1934, entry.

6 . F. Neave, "New Ways to Waddington," 40.

7. Forde, "Hints on the Use of the Rope," June 1927, 4.

8. F. Neave, "New Ways to Waddington," 40.

9. Forde, "Hints on the Use of the Rope," Aug. 1927, 4.

10. Forde, "Hints on the Use of the Rope," Sept. 1927, 4.

11. Forde, "Hints on the Use of the Rope," Sept. 1927, 4.

12. Forde, "Hints on the Use of the Rope," May 1927, 4.

13. F. Neave, "New Ways to Waddington," 40.

14. F. Neave, "New Ways to Waddington," 40.

15. R. Neave, interview.

16. F. Neave, "New Ways to Waddington," 41.

17. Forde, "Hints on the Use of the Rope," Aug. 1927, 4.

18. R. Neave, interview.

19. F. Neave, *Waddington Expedition Diary*, June 27, 1934, entry.

20. F. Neave, "New Ways to Waddington," 41.

21. R. Neave, interview.

22. F. Neave, "New Ways to Waddington," 41.

23. Forde, "Hints on the Use of the Rope," Sept. 1927, 4.

24. R. Neave, interview.

25. R. Neave, interview.

26. F. Neave, *Waddington Expedition Diary*, June 28, 1934, entry.

27. F. Neave, "New Ways to Waddington," 42.

28. R. Neave, interview.

29. F. Neave, "New Ways to Waddington," 43.

30. R. Neave, interview.

31. F. Neave, "New Ways to Waddington," 43.

32. F. Neave, "New Ways to Waddington," 43–44.

33. F. Neave, "New Ways to Waddington," 45.

Chapter 8

1. E. Whymper, *Scrambles Amongst the Alps*, 322.

2. E. Whymper, *Scrambles Amongst the Alps*, 322.

3. E. Whymper, *Scrambles Amongst the Alps*, 324.

4. Carter, "Fatal Accident on Mt. Waddington," 46.

5. P. Munday, "Old Ways to Waddington."

6. P. Munday, "Old Ways to Waddington."

7. P. Munday, "Old Ways to Waddington."

8. Scott, *Pushing the Limits*, 121.

9. Carter, "Editorial," 1.

10. Carter, "An Expedition," 4.

11. Scott, *Pushing the Limits*, 122.

12. Carter, "The Summer Camp," 1.

13. Carter, "Still a Mystery," 4.

14. Scott, *Pushing the Limits*, 122.

15. Dalgleish, "Source of the Toba River," 56.

16. Dalgleish, "Source of the Toba River," 59, 62.

17. Dalgleish, "Source of the Toba River," 56.

18. Carter, "Fatal Accident on Mt. Waddington," 46.

19. Scott, *Pushing the Limits*, 114.

20. Carter, "Fatal Accident on Mt. Waddington," 46.

21. Forde, "Hints on the Use of the Rope," May 1927, 3.

22. Carter, "The Fatal Accident on Mt. Waddington," 49.

23. Carter, "Fatal Accident on Mt. Waddington," 49–50.

24. Carter, "Fatal Accident on Mt. Waddington," 49–50.

Chapter 9

1. Carter, "Fatal Accident on Mt. Waddington," 55.

2. Scott, *Pushing the Limits*, 114.

3. Carter, "Fatal Accident on Mt. Waddington," 55.

4. D. Munday, "High Peaks of the Coast Range," 1.

5. D. Munday, "Mt. Waddington, 1934," 24.

6. D. Munday, "Mt. Waddington, 1934," 25.

7. D. Munday, "Mt. Waddington, 1934," 24.

8. D. Munday, "Mt. Waddington, 1934," 25.

9. D. Munday, "Mt. Waddington, 1934," 26.

10. D. Munday, "Mt. Waddington, 1934," 26.

11. D. Munday, "Mt. Waddington, 1934," 27.

12. D. Munday, "Mt. Waddington, 1934," 28.

13. D. Munday, "Mt. Waddington, 1934," 28.

14. D. Munday, "Mt. Waddington, 1934," 28.

15. D. Munday, "Mt. Waddington, 1934," 28.

16. D. Munday, "Mt. Waddington, 1934," 29.

17. D. Munday, "Mt. Waddington, 1934," 29.

18. Scott, *Pushing the Limits*, 113.

Chapter 10

1. D. Munday, "Historical Sketch of Mt. Waddington Region," 105–6.

2. Betts, "Lecture by Don Munday," 1.

3. Scott, *Pushing the Limits*, 114.

4. Jordan, "Mount Waddington," 1.

5. Jordan, "Mount Waddington," 1.

6. Leonard, "Can Mt. Waddington Be Climbed?," 28.

7. Leonard, "Can Mt. Waddington Be Climbed?," 35.

8. Leonard, "Can Mt. Waddington Be Climbed?," 36.

9. Voge, "Climbs in the Waddington Region," 29.

10. Dobson, "Mount Waddington Expedition," Aug. 1936, 3–4.
11. Weissner, "First Ascent of Mt. Waddington," 9.
12. Voge, "Climbs in the Waddington Region," 29–30.
13. Weissner, "First Ascent of Mt. Waddington," 9.
14. Jordan, "Mount Waddington Expedition," 2.
15. Dobson, "Mount Waddington Expedition," Aug. 1936, 3.
16. Dobson, "Mount Waddington Expedition," Nov. 1936, 2.
17. Weissner, "First Ascent of Mt. Waddington," 11.
18. Dobson, "Mount Waddington Expedition," Nov. 1936, 2.
19. Dobson, "Mount Waddington Expedition," Nov. 1936, 3–4.
20. Scott, *Pushing the Limits*, 116.
21. Betts, "Mr. and Mrs. Munday's Lecture," 1.

Afterword

1. Culbert, *Coast Mountains Trilogy*, 41.
2. Barman, "Cascadia Once Upon a Time," 91.
3. Muir, *Mountains of California*, 31.
4. Muir, *Mountains of California*, 31.
5. Muir, *Mountains of California*, 39–40.
6. Adams and Muir, *Yosemite and the Sierra Nevada*, 67.
7. Dart, *Mountaineering and the Humanities*, 63.
8. Dart, *Mountaineering and the Humanities*, 45.
9. Dart, *Mountaineering and the Humanities*, 45.

BIBLIOGRAPHY

Adams, Ansel (photography), and John Muir (text). *Yosemite and the Sierra Nevada.* Houghton Mifflin Company, 1948.

Barman, Jean. "Cascadia Once Upon a Time." In *Cascadia: The Elusive Utopia*, edited by Douglas Todd, 89-104. Ronsdale Press, 2008.

Betts, J.N., ed. "An Attempt on Mt. Waddington." *The B.C. Mountaineer* 11, no. 6 (June 1934): 3.

Betts, J.N., ed. "Lecture by Don Munday: March 15." *The B.C. Mountaineer* 13, no. 3 (March 1935): 1.

Betts, J.N., ed. "Mount Seymour Trip: May 19–20." *The B.C. Mountaineer* 11, no. 6 (June 1934): 2.

Betts, J.N., ed. "Mr. and Mrs. Munday's Lecture." *The B.C. Mountaineer* 13, no. 4 (April 1935): 1.

Betts, J.N., ed. "Red-Snow and Ice-Worms: Extract from an article by G.H. Wailes." *The B.C. Mountaineer* 13, no. 5 (May 1935): 3–4.

Bridge, Kathryn. *A Passion for Mountains: The Lives of Don and Phyllis Munday.* Rocky Mountain Books, 2006.

Carter, Neal M., ed. "Editorial." *The B.C. Mountaineer* 4, no. 2 (April 1926): 1.

Carter, Neal M., ed. "An Expedition." *The B.C. Mountaineer* 4, no. 4 (June 1926): 4.

Carter, Neal M. "The Fatal Accident on Mt. Waddington." *Canadian Alpine Journal* xxii (1934): 46–55.

Carter, Neal M., ed. "Still a Mystery." *The B.C. Mountaineer* 4, no. 5 (July 1926): 4.

Carter, Neal M., ed., "The Summer Camp." *The B.C. Mountaineer* 4, no. 5 (July 1926): 1.

Clark, Ronald. *The Day the Rope Broke: The Story of a Great Victorian Tragedy.* Secker & Warburg, 1965.

Clark, Ronald. *The Victorian Mountaineers.* B.T. Batsford, 1953.

Cooper, A.J.O., ed. "The Relation of Skiing to Mountaineering." *The B.C. Mountaineer* 12, no. 7 (February 1931): 1–2.

Culbert, Dick. *The Coast Mountains Trilogy: Mountain Poems 1957–1971.* Illustrated by Arnold Shives. Tricouni Press, 2009.

Dalgleish, Alec. "The Source of the Toba River." *Canadian Alpine Journal* XXII (1934): 56–62.

Dart, Ron. *Mountaineering and the Humanities.* Illustrated by Arnold Shives. Serratus Press, 2007.

Dobson, Bill. "Mount Waddington Expedition." *The B.C. Mountaineer* 14, no. 8 (August 1936): 3–4.

Dobson, Bill. "Mount Waddington Expedition." *The B.C. Mountaineer* 14, no. 11 (November 1936): 2–4.

Forde, J.P. "Hints on the Use of the Rope in Mountain Climbing." *The B.C. Mountaineer* 5, no. 1 (March 1927): 4.

Forde, J.P. "Hints on the Use of the Rope in Mountain Climbing" *The B.C. Mountaineer* 5, no. 3 (May 1927). Installment of article by J.P. Forde originally published in the *Canadian Alpine Journal*: 3–4.

Forde, J.P. "Hints on the Use of the Rope in Mountain Climbing." *The B.C. Mountaineer* 5, no. 4 (June 1927). Installment of article by J.P. Forde originally published in the *Canadian Alpine Journal*: 3–4.

Forde, J.P. "Hints on the Use of the Rope in Mountain Climbing." *The B.C. Mountaineer* 5, no. 6 (August 1927). Installment of article by J.P. Forde originally published in the *Canadian Alpine Journal*: 4.

Forde, J.P. "Hints on the Use of the Rope in Mountain Climbing" *The B.C. Mountaineer* 5, no. 7 (September 1927). Installment of article by J.P. Forde originally published in the *Canadian Alpine Journal*: 4.

Foster, H.D., ed. "Invading the Mountains of Bute Inlet." *The B.C. Mountaineer* 3, no. 8 (October 1925): 4.

Foster, H.D., ed. "Photographic Exhibition." *The B.C. Mountaineer* 4, no. 1 (March 1926): 1–2.

Hall, Henry S., Jr. "The 1934 Attempts on Mount Waddington." *American Alpine Journal* 2, no. 3 (1935): 298–306.

Hall, Henry S., Jr. "The Coast Range from the North and East." *Canadian Alpine Journal* XXI (1933): 93–110.

Henry, Tom. *The Good Company: An Affectionate History of the Union Steamships*. Harbour Publishing, 1994.

Huggard, John, ed. "Lecture on Mystery Mountain." *The B.C. Mountaineer* 5, no. 2 (April 1927): 2.

Johnson, Peter. *A Not-So-Savage Land: The Art and Times of Frederick Whymper 1838–1901*. Heritage House, 2018.

Jordan, M., ed. "Mount Waddington." *The B.C. Mountaineer* 15, no. 6 (June 1936): 1.

Jordan, M., ed. "Mount Waddington Expedition." *The B.C. Mountaineer* 15, no. 7 (July 1936): 2–3.

Leslie, Susan, ed. *In the Western Mountains: Early Mountaineering in British Columbia*. Provincial Archives of British Columbia, 1980.

Leonard, Richard. "Can Mt. Waddington Be Climbed?" *Canadian Alpine Journal* XXIII (1936): 28–36.

Lunn, Sir Arnold. *The Bernese Oberland*. Eyre & Spottiswoode, 1958.

McCoubrey, A.A. "A Purcell Pilgrimage." *Canadian Alpine Journal* XVIII (1929): 74–81.

Muir, John. *The Mountains of California*. Ten Speed Press, 1977. Originally published in 1894.

Munday, Don. "The Apex of the Coast Range." *Canadian Alpine Journal* XVI (1928): 1–15.

Munday, Don. "Exploration in the Coast Range." *The B.C. Mountaineer* 4, no. 6 (August 1926): 4.

Munday, Don. "Exploration in the Coast Range." *Canadian Alpine Journal* XVI (1928): 121–40.

Munday, Don. "The Heart of the Coast Range." *The B.C. Mountaineer* 6, no. 10 (December 1928): 3–4.

Munday, Don. "High Peaks of the Coast Range." *Canadian Alpine Journal* XVII (1934): 1–23.

Munday, Don. "Historical Sketch of Mt. Waddington Region." *Canadian Alpine Journal* xviii (1930): 98–106.

Munday, Don. "Mt. Arrowsmith." *The B.C. Mountaineer* 3, no. 5 (July 1925): 3.

Munday, Don. "Mt. Waddington." *Canadian Alpine Journal* xvii (1929): 1–13.

Munday, Don. "Mt. Waddington, 1934." *Canadian Alpine Journal* xvii (1934): 24–31.

Munday, Don. "Mystery Mountain." *The B.C. Mountaineer* 5, no. 10 (December 1927): 1–2.

Munday, Don. "Ski-Climbs in the Coast Range." *Canadian Alpine Journal* xix (1931): 101–11.

Munday, Don. *The Unknown Mountain*, 2nd Edition. The Mountaineers, 1975.

Munday, Phyllis. "First Ascent of Mt. Robson by Lady Members." *Canadian Alpine Journal* xiv (1924): 68–74.

Munday, Phyllis. "Old Ways to Waddington." Introduced by Dr. Neal M. Carter. 1964. Item AAAC4001, Accession number: T4293. BC Archives. Cassette.

Nauticapedia: The Virtual Maritime Museum of Western North America. "Chelohsin." Record creator: John M. MacFarlane, 2020. Accessed October 2024. https://nauticapedia.ca/dbase/Query/Shiplist5 .php?&name=Chelohsin&id=3546&Page=1&input=Chelohsin.

Neave, Ferris. *1934 Mt. Waddington Expedition Diary*. Whyte Museum Archives of the Canadian Rockies, Banff, Alberta.

Neave, Ferris. "Climbing at Banff." *Canadian Alpine Journal* xviii (1929): 92–95.

Neave, Ferris. "In Memoriam: Alexander Addison McCoubrey 1885–1942." In *Manitoba Climbers: A Century of Stories from the Birthplace of the Alpine Club of Canada*, edited by Christine Mazur, Simon Statkewich, and David Ralkoff, 77–81. Alpine Club of Canada, Manitoba Section, 2006.

Neave, Ferris. "New Ways to Waddington." *Canadian Alpine Journal* xvii (1934): 32–45.

Neave, Ferris. "Spring Snows of the Yoho." *Canadian Alpine Journal* xxi (1933): 122–27.

Neave, Roger. "Roger Neave Interview." Interviewed by Susan Leslie. 1979. Item AAAB3944, Accession number: T3551. BC Archives. Cassette.

O'Connor, Joe. "The Search for B.C.'s Mystery Mountain: Experts Said It Didn't Exist—Then Don and Phyllis Munday Found It." *National Post.* July 2, 2018. https://nationalpost.com/news/canada/the-search-for-b-c-s-mystery-mountain-experts-said-it-didnt-exist-then-don-and-phyllis-munday-found-it.

Oreskovic, Susanna. *Expedition to Mystery Mountain: Adventures of a Bushwacking, Knickerbocker-wearing Woman.* Walnut Tree Press, 2021.

Parker, Gil. "Roger Neave: Pioneer Mountaineer." In *Manitoba Climbers: A Century of Stories from the Birthplace of the Alpine Club of Canada*, edited by Christine Mazur, Simon Statkewich, and David Ralkoff, 42–46. Alpine Club of Canada, Manitoba Section, 2006.

Ricker, Karl. "Dr. Ferris Neave, F.R.S.C." In *Manitoba Climbers: A Century of Stories from the Birthplace of the Alpine Club of Canada*, edited by Christine Mazur, Simon Statkewich, and David Ralkoff, 47–69. Alpine Club of Canada, Manitoba Section, 2006.

Robinson, Bestor. "Mount Waddington—1935." *Sierra Club Bulletin* XXI, no. 1 (February 1936): 1–11.

Ruskin, John. *Modern Painters, Volume IV: Of Mountain Beauty.* Dana Estes & Company, 1903.

Scott, Andrew. *The Encyclopedia of Raincoast Place Names: A Complete Reference to Coastal British Columbia.* Harbour Publishing, 2009.

Scott, Chic. *Pushing the Limits: The Story of Canadian Mountaineering.* Rocky Mountain Books, 2000.

Sherman, Paddy. *Cloud Walkers: Six Climbs on Major Canadian Peaks.* MacMillan, 1965.

Skelton, Kate. "Archival Highlights: Malcolm Geddes." The Whyte. May 17, 2021. https://www.whyte.org/post/archival-highlights-malcolm-geddes.

Smythe, F.S. *Edward Whymper.* Hodder and Stoughton, 1940.

Smythe, F.S. *The Spirit of the Hills.* Hodder and Stoughton, 1941. Originally published in 1935.

Spouse, F.A., ed. "Mt. Waddington Conquered." *The B.C. Mountaineer* 6, no. 6 (August 1928): 4.

Taylor, A., ed. "The Accident on Little Goat." *The B.C. Mountaineer* 5, no. 1 (March 1927): 2–3.

Twain, Mark. *A Tramp Abroad.* Edited by Roy Blount, Jr. The Library of America, 2010. Originally published in 1921 by the Mark Twain Company.

Voge, Hervey. "Climbs in the Waddington Region—1936." *Sierra Club Bulletin* xxii, no. 1 (February 1937): 29–37.

Watson, Sir Norman, and Edward J. King. *Round Mystery Mountain: A Ski Adventure.* Longmans, Green and Co., 1935.

Weissner, Fritz H. "The First Ascent of Mount Waddington." *Canadian Alpine Journal* xxiv (1936): 9–17.

Wheeler, Arthur O. "Rogers Pass at the Summit of the Selkirks." *Canadian Alpine Journal* xvii (1929): 38–52.

Whymper, Edward. *Scrambles Amongst the Alps.* Century Publishing, 1985. First published in Great Britain in 1871 by John Murray (Publishers) Ltd.

Whymper, Frederick, *Travel and Adventure in the Territory of Alaska, formerly Russian America—now ceded to the United States—and in various other parts of the North Pacific.* John Murray, Albemarle Street, 1869.

Williams, Judith. *Raincoast Chronicles 24: Cougar Companions: Bute Inlet Country and the Legendary Schnarrs.* Harbour Publishing, 2019.

Woods, Don M. "Sierra Climbers on Waddington." *Canadian Alpine Journal* xxiii (1936): 23–27.

ILLUSTRATION CREDITS

63	Image E-04959 courtesy of BC Archives
65	Image I-68085 courtesy of BC Archives
69	Image H-03440 courtesy of BC Archives
75	Image I-51584 courtesy of BC Archives
76–77	Image E-04954 courtesy of BC Archives
81	Image I-51586 courtesy of BC Archives
86	Courtesy of *Canadian Alpine Journal*
87	Courtesy of *Canadian Alpine Journal*
110	Image 6703 courtesy of the Museum at Campbell River
145	NVMA, 37:018
159	NVMA, 37:034
165	Image 15516 courtesy of the Museum at Campbell River
166	NVMA, 37:011
168	Image I-61647 courtesy of BC Archives
170	NVMA, 37:025
176	NVMA, 37:026
177	NVMA, 37:020
179	NVMA, 37:005
180	NVMA, 37:027
181	NVMA, 37:010
182	NVMA, 37:008
184	NVMA, 37:092
185	NVMA, 37:023
187	NVMA, 37:022
189	NVMA, 37:021

INDEX

Page numbers of photographs are in bold.

Dart, Ron, 197–98
Dentiform, Mount, 123
Dobson, William, **181**, 183, 186, 188
Dolmage, Victor, 29
Douglas, Lord Francis, 15, 17, 147
Drinnan, Andy, 38

Eichorn, Jules, 178
entomology, 62

Forbes, James David, 13, 16
Forde, J.P., 126, 130–31, 135–39, 141
Foster, H.D., 32, 152
Foster, W.W., 180
Franklin Glacier, 50, 57–60, **61**, 62, 64, 68, **69**, 73–74, **76**, **77**, 79–80, 97, 99, 117, 156, **166**, 167, **179**, **182**
Franklin River, 50–51, 57, 59, 74, 156, 166
Fury Gap, 62, **63**, 67, 74, 77, 97
Fyles, Tom, 152, 154–55

Geddes, Malcolm Daniel, 67
Geddes, Mount, 67, 123
Geographic Board of Canada, 30, 58, 66
Geographical Journal, The, 177
George, Hereford Brooke, 15
Gillen, Denver, 182
Glendale Cannery, 57–59, 94, 150, 156, 166
golden age of mountaineering, 13–16, 18, 124, 163, 193
Grassi, Lawrence, **181**, 183
"Great Glacier, Bute Inlet", 20, **23**, 119, 127
Grouse Mountain, 36, 56
Grouse Mountain Resort Company, 55–56

Hadow, Douglas, 15, 17, 147
Hall, Henry S., Jr., 79–80, **81**, 82, 99, 123, 152, 165–67, 178, 180
Harvard Mountaineering Club, 180

ABOUT THE AUTHOR

It was while riding a motorcycle across British Columbia for over a decade that Trevor Marc Hughes began writing about the history of his home province in *Nearly 40 on the 37* and *Zero Avenue to Peace Park*. He then developed late B.C. naturalist Hamilton Mack Laing's account of his 1915 motorcycle travels across the United States for *Riding the Continent*. Researching and writing *Capturing the Summit: Hamilton Mack Laing and the Mount Logan Expedition of 1925* led him to further explore mountaineering records and archives in Canada. *The Final Spire* is the result.

Growing up in Victoria, Trevor then moved to Vancouver soon after high school graduation. There he worked as a television actor, arts broadcaster, and freelance writer. He is currently the non-fiction editor and video segment producer for *The British Columbia Review*. www.trevormarchughes.ca